Castleknob

FIRST IN A SERIES ENTITLED THE KUDZU KLAN

Cynthia Cochran Kinard

New Harbor Press

RAPID CITY, SD

Kinard/New Harbor Press
1601 Mt. Rushmore Rd, Ste 3288
Rapid City, SD 57701
www.NewHarborPress.com

Ordering Information:
Quantity sales. Special discounts are available on quantity purchases by corporations, associations, and others. For details, contact the "Special Sales Department" at the address above.

Castleknob / Cynthia Cochran Kinard. 2nd ed.
ISBN 978-1-63357-469-4

Dedication

This book is dedicated to my mother, Eleanor Cochran, who instilled in me, at an early age, her great love of reading. At the writing of this book, she is 84 years old and still lending books from her vast library. She can read entire novels in a day and retains most of what she reads. I attribute her marvelous memory and 20/20 vision to the fact that she has kept those muscles exercised with her daily reading. In addition, because she is so well-read, she can converse with anyone at any level.

The fact that I am a Christian is a direct result of my mother's influence, as well. Therefore, I am able to pass along that strong faith in my writing. There was never a question about to whom I would dedicate this book. I owe the fact that I am an author and avid reader entirely to my mother.

With Gratitude

magination, coupled with real life experiences, were the seeds from which this book sprang. Therefore, those I met in my life who contributed to this storyline are simply too many to mention. I am thankful to all of those who helped shape and form my life, resulting in the work which is about to unfold before you. There are those who especially stand out in my mind, however.

The first is my father, who loved these mountains and instilled that love in me, as well. He taught me to love the old ways and antiques. He also showed me that older family members have so much to offer the younger ones, if they will only listen. He planted in my heart a strong love for animals and to care well for them. So much of this storyline stems from the richness of his life and the memories with which he left me. He was my favorite person in the world and his memory will always stay fresh and vivid as his influence is woven throughout the following pages. I could never thank him enough for all that he taught me.

My dear friend, Ola Norman, encouraged me heavily in my writing and kept back-up copies of my manuscript (just in case). She gave me my first computer, so I was off and running with my writing at last! She is another one who lent me many books and now does this for a living as a librarian. She influenced me to seek a publisher and I am very grateful for her part in this writing.

Betty Richardson and Helen Ray, two sisters who attend our church and have become like family to my husband and me, were willing to give of their time and proof the manuscript. Their love of Christ is reflected in their giving spirits and I am thankful they gave to this effort and found the book absorbing.

My husband read the first few chapters I wrote of the sequel to this book entitled, *The Sang Hunters,* and said I had captured the spirit of his beloved mountains. He encouraged me to continue— and as I wrote, I realized that I must back up and write the story of what brought the McKaine family to the mountains in the first place. The confidence my husband placed in me by those few words inspired me to continue. He has my undying gratitude.

There were those who faithfully stayed by my side through the long days and nights of writing. They literally have been with me every step of the way and kept me well satisfied with their devoted company. To arise from my computer meant stepping over their warm, furry bodies. Therefore, my beloved dogs played a vital role and I appreciate them for that.

Last of all, the great God about whom I write in these pages is real and true and very present in my life. This may be a work of fiction, but it hopefully portrays how life could be if we would only trust Him. It is how it is for me and without Him I could not have written this work or have even taken my next breath! For all of the gifts that He so freely gave me, I am eternally grateful.

Chapter One

The weight of the world hung like a mantle on the slender shoulders of the young girl who sat at the window. With her left cheek and temple pressed against the cold pane, Jessie McKaine sat hoping that its coolness would ease the hot throbbing in her head. The fierce storm outside showed no signs of letting up and the fierce storm inside seemed the same.

Distractedly, Jessie watched the raindrops, little rivulets making their way down the glass, then out of the range of her vision. Her mother's shallow breathing and the raindrops had become one in her mind, and soon the sound of the breathing, like the raindrops, would run its course and be no more.

How this could be, Jessie could not fathom. How could things have gone so wrong? But, then, in the pit of her stomach, Jessie knew that this time of child birthing she had feared this very thing and now it was coming to pass. Jessie had prayed until the stream of words had run dry. For days she had prayed, unceasingly, no matter that she was weary beyond belief. God seemed so silent, dreadfully silent, but in Jessie's heart she knew the time was at hand.

Where was her father? Why was he not here being strong for them all? Jessie's throat choked and she swallowed back the hot tears. Even while she was controlling one part of her body, however, her eyes had mutinied and the tears flowed, keeping pace with the raindrops.

Jessie's shoulders heaved and the young, straight back bent at last as the teenager gave way to her grief. How long she gave vent to her emotions, she had no way of knowing, but suddenly through the haze of her thinking the realization that her mother's breathing had changed, broke through to her.

Whirling around, the young girl heard a sharp intake of breath and then saw a look of peace and radiance cross her mother's face, obliterating the pain and suffering that had been etched there. Crossing quickly to her mother's side, Jessie grasped the thin hand in her own young, eager ones and whispered, "Mom...."

Though Kathleen McKaine continued to look at the ceiling as if she could not tear her eyes away, it was obvious that she had heard her daughter. She took a deep breath and a brilliant smile lit her face. Jessie stared as if transfixed. The happiness on her mother's face was a sight to behold.

"Jessie, is that you?"

Jessie's voice threatened to stay hidden in her throat. Such was her awe of her mother's look, but a small, childlike voice whispered, "Yes, Mama...."

"Jessie, you must listen to me. Do you know how much I love you?"

Again, the little voice, this time laced with tears, "Yes, Mama, I love you too...so very much."

A tear made its way from her mother's eye into the fever dampened hair. But her voice was stronger now and tinged with a tired excitement.

"Jessie, I don't have much longer."

"No, Mama...."

"Jessie, darling...denying it won't change anything. Besides... He has told me that it is time. I will be with Him...soon."

Jessie's weeping increased, but she struggled to hang on.

"Darling, Jessie, so much is depending on you. You are so young to be saddled...with so much, but you must be strong... and courageous. God will help you."

"Why isn't He helping now, then?" Jessie cried out almost angrily.

Her mother seemed less strong and her voice was softer still when next she spoke.

"Darling, it is not for us...to question God's timing. He has appointed a time for each of us to go be with Him. This is simply...my time. You must accept that...."

Weeping softly, Jessie laid her face against her mother's shoulder and whispered, "I'm sorry, Mama."

"Jessie, I am talking to you this way because today you must become an adult. You must shoulder...adult responsibilities. It is I who am sorry for that, but your father...he must have been captured...or else he is in hiding."

Kathleen looked to the side as her mind wandered off and Jessie's heart clutched to think how very much her mother must want her husband to be by her side at this moment.

"You must believe that he is alive...and will come for you soon," Kathleen breathed once more, as she focused her mind and lay gathering strength for what she had yet to say, praying as she did so that God would grant her life long enough to get it said.

Jessie's heart filled with fresh pain, thinking of her father who would not be here for his wife's final moments. How grieved he would be! Oh, it was all wrong! Jessie's heart threatened to burst with the pain of it!

Her mother had rallied and was speaking again. "Jessie, you must keep everyone together. The authorities will probably come and try to place you in foster care. You must not be separated! Stay together...for your dad. Flee if you must, but stay together."

The force of her words sapped so much of her remaining strength, but Kathleen had to get it all said.

"And, Jessie. Stay away from Sean! Don't let any of the children go with him. Jessie, understand! Don't leave any of the children even alone with him. And...don't let him know if you have to flee. Whatever you do, don't let him know where you are going!"

Fear caught at Jessie's heart at the sound of her mother's words. Kathleen was spent from the emphasis of her statements and Jessie began to wonder if her mother had slipped into unconsciousness again.

In a much weaker voice she continued, "Jessie, you have been a good girl. You are mature for your age and I know I can trust you. And...I know you can trust God. He will see you through. Listen to Him....Now, please get the others."

Having stayed so long in one position without having realized it, Jessie was surprised to discover how stiff she was. She threw her shoulders back, however, and went woodenly toward the door to do what needed to be done.

Six somber faces watched as their big sister, Jessie, quietly tiptoed to their mother's side. Grandpa, standing between the two oldest children, seemed not to understand. Kathleen McKaine's eyes were still fixed upon the ceiling and the radiant look was still upon her drawn features.

Jessie leaned down and whispered through a throat that seemed too thick for words, "Mama...."

It was a full minute before Kathleen seemed able to tear her eyes from that spot on the ceiling and when she did, twin tears coursed down onto her dampened pillow.

Kathleen's voice was full of emotion when at last she spoke, "Send them to me, Jessie, dear."

Jessie drew back and motioned for Ryler, one of the two-year-old twins. He reached for Tyler, and together they approached the bed, not understanding why everything was so hushed and still. Mama had lain in this bed for days and they had missed her so and now they were to see her.

Jessie smiled weakly at them to encourage them, though she knew they did not understand the tears streaming down her face.

Two little pairs of arms gently hugged their mother and two little voices whispered almost simultaneously, "Me ub oo, Mama."

"I love you too, my darlings. You must do as Mama asks. Obey your sister, Jessie...for Mama...."

With wide eyes, the little boys nodded at their mother, embraced her once more with their chubby little arms and then toddled back to stand in line.

Little red-headed Katy, namesake for her mother, moved timidly to the bed. At four, she knew enough to understand that something was dreadfully wrong and she almost trembled in her fright. Her mother was almost the same color as her pillows and she abstractedly thought of her crayons. At four, she was already quite the little artist and her child mind realized that her mother's skin was not the same as her flesh-colored crayon.

Her small hand reached out to finger her mother's damp hair and she saw, to her dismay, fresh tears roll from her mother's eyes onto the damp pillow.

"My little Kathleen. You are Mama's brave little girl and I love you so much." Kathleen McKaine's head sunk deeper into the pillow, as if the weight of her feelings was too much for her.

Little Kathleen continued to stroke her mother's hair and face and her little back straightened as if she was already trying to be the brave little girl that her mother wanted her to be. Finally, turning slightly to face her once more, her mother breathed, "Katy...you must mind Jessie. She will take care of you. Be good to her for me...and help her all you can. And...always, wait for your father. He is going to need your love."

Kathleen lifted a weak arm to hug her daughter and Katy's little face crumpled with her emotions. Micah helped Katy down from the stool and Josh moved to his mother's side. It was obvious that he was trying to be brave and not cry, but silent tears were making their way down his cheeks.

"Josh, my love. You must be daddy's little man. You must help Jessie in any way she asks. She is going to need you and you must mind her...for me."

"I will Mama...." Josh's answer was barely audible. Then he threw his arms around his mother's neck and hugged her ever so gently and though those present heard nothing, his mother heard his whispered, "I love you," and her heart was rent even more.

Micah looked at his older sister Sarah and then being the young gentleman that he was, deferred his place to her. Sarah was openly weeping as she handed the baby, Annie, to Jessie. Her mute lips worked with all the words that she wanted to say.

Her heart breaking, she thought that her mother perhaps could not focus her eyes well anymore and that the things in her heart might not get to be signed. Still, she extended her thumb, index and little finger toward her mother in the sign, "I love you."

Then Sarah's attempt at control vanished as her mother returned the sign, weak though she was. Kathleen used a lot of her remaining strength to say weakly, "Help, Jessie." And, "I am depending on you."

Micah hurried into place as he saw the strength leaving his mother's body. At thirteen, he was a responsible young man and very intuitive. He grasped his mother's hand and was appalled at the weakness he felt there. He somehow knew that she was holding on by an act of sheer will and with all his heart, he wished that he could infuse some of his energy and strength into her body. He loved her so and now they were going to lose her. "How could this be?" his mind roared.

"Micah...I love you, son." Kathleen was fighting for every breath now. Sweat beads had gathered on her upper lip and were running down the tiny smile lines on each side of her mouth. "You must be...the man...of the...family...now."

Kathleen had closed her eyes as if this would give her more strength. "Until...your father...returns."

"Mom, you know I will. I'll do anything for you...anything, Mom." Micah breathed these words out with such urgency. "Mom, we all love you so much..." Micah's voice broke as he considered his next words. "You've been the best Mom ever," and the teenager laid his blond head on his mother's breast and wept.

Jessie gently placed her hand on Micah's shoulder. He turned slowly to rejoin the others. Grabbing Grandpa's hand, Jessie placed it in her mother's own weak one. Kathleen looked up at her father one last time, her eyes filled with a special brand of love. "Good-bye, Poppa, I love you," she whispered.

As Jessie motioned, the two oldest turned to leave the room, ushering the little ones out as they went. Grandpa ambled along behind them looking more confused than ever and Jessie's heart went out to him. His daughter was dying and he didn't even comprehend it.

Turning back to the bed, Jessie realized just what an enormous strain these "good-byes" had been for her mother. Even so, the tiny rasps that were now her mother's breathing were a new source of surprise, and Jessie's shoulders slumped as she was forced to face the inevitable.

Jessie had to lean in close to her mother's mouth to catch the next words, "Jess...the baby."

Placing Annie gently at her mother's side, Jessie thought that she could not take any more as her mother turned her head slightly to place a gentle kiss on the sleeping baby's forehead, crooning her love to it. Then her mother turned and, once again, looked at the ceiling. She smiled a weak smile and peace descended onto her strained features, relaxing them even in the face of death, into such a radiant beauty.

"Take good care of Poppa...he was such a wise man... before...."

"Remember...stay together...stay a family...and wait for your dad."

All of this effort to speak took its final toll, "I will wait for you...I love you all...." and with that Kathleen McKaine spoke her last words.

Chapter Two

Sean McAllister stood in the kitchen of the McKaine home. He felt little pity for the children who had lost their mother, his sister. "Served her right!" His evil mind thought. "She always was a goody two-shoes and she married a man just like her."

He glanced around at the old man who was sitting and staring into space. "I'm sure not going to be saddled with the old man like Kathleen was. He's not my father anyway. The State will have to look after him." Sean's thoughts continued.

At that moment, Sarah entered the room with a screaming Annie.

"Can't you keep that kid quiet?" Sean yelled.

Sarah began to prepare the formula with one hand while she held the baby close with the other. Sean reached out and grabbed her arm, causing formula to spill on the stove and floor. "You may be dumb, but I know you're not deaf! Now keep that kid quiet!"

Jessie walked in at that moment and moved like lightning to intercept Micah as he made a lunge at his uncle. "No, Micah! Let it go!"

Sean turned, curling his lips into a sneer, "That's right, boy! You'd better listen to your sister. You touch me and it will be something you'll never forget."

Micah jerked out of Jessie's hold on him and stalked from the room. Jessie's heart went out to him. She knew he was wishing desperately to be more than his thirteen years right now.

Jessie quickly signed to the frightened Sarah to take the baby into another room and she would finish preparing the bottle. Sarah lost no time in exiting the room. Jessie stooped to clean the floor of the spilled formula and then she prepared the bottle.

Sean watched her movements, thinking once again just how pretty his two nieces were becoming. No, that was not quite correct. They were more than pretty. Sarah was becoming a downright beauty. Pity, she had that disability, but it might come in useful sometime in the near future.

Her mind working furiously, Jessie finished the bottle and went to find Sarah and the baby. With Annie still screaming, it was not difficult to do so. Sarah was rocking her in their parents' bedroom. Jessie felt a fresh wave of pain as she entered the room. She brushed it aside and focused on the task at hand, however.

Annie had been such a good baby the first three weeks, but in the week since her mother's death, she had taken to screaming on a regular basis. Jessie felt surely that she had just sensed how upset everyone else was and was reacting to it. At least she hoped that was all. The last thing they needed was for the authorities to think there was anything wrong.

Sean had accepted the role of temporary guardian or they would already have been placed in foster care. Jessie was thankful for that much, but she remembered her mother's words and knew this could not last for long. She had confided in Sarah and Micah what her mother had said about not leaving any of the children even alone in the same room with him, so the three of them had been vigilant about the younger ones.

The time had come to act, however. They must leave soon, only Jessie did not know where to go. Her head throbbed from all the crying and thinking she had been doing, but still no solution had presented itself.

Leaving Sarah with a now content Annie, Jessie took a deep breath for courage and headed back to the kitchen. Thankfully,

Sean was no longer there. She heard the sound of his old truck starting up and glanced out the window at the flat Georgia landscape in time to see him peeling off. She spotted Josh sitting on a stump, silhouetted by the setting sun. The twins and Katy were taking turns swinging. Micah was leaning against a gnarled oak tree not far away, dejection and defeat written clearly in his stance.

Jessie turned with a sigh and walked toward her grandfather, who was staring out the dining room window. Suddenly, she wished she were a little girl again and there was someone taking care of her. She dropped to her knees in front of her grandfather and laid her aching head in his lap. "God, help us." She breathed for the hundredth time.

"Grandpa, what are we going to do?" She said out loud. "We have to leave here. Where are we going to go? Please tell me, Grandpa. I need wisdom right now in the worst sort of way. Tell me, Grandpa, where can we go?"

"We could always go to Charlie's."

It was her grandfather's voice! Jessie jerked her head up and looked into his eyes. There was recognition there! Miraculously, there was recognition there!

"Grandpa!" Jessie exclaimed as she struggled upright on her knees. "Grandpa, you know me!"

"Of course, I know you, Jessie," Kevin McAllister stated, as if this was the most normal thing in the world.

Jessie jumped to her feet and threw her arms around her grandfather. "Thank you, God, thank you!" played through her mind as joy coursed through her being.

She was so ecstatic about the fact that her grandfather was lucid that she almost missed what he had said. Then it came back to her and it made all the sense in the world.

Her great-uncle Charlie was her grandfather's brother. He was a recluse who lived in the remote mountains of North Carolina. Her father had taken her mother, Sarah, Micah, Josh and herself when Jessie was nine years old, on a camping trip to the mountains where they had camped on Charlie McAllister's land. Jessie remembered the wild beauty of the place and their one meeting with their uncle Charlie. Would he consider helping them find a place to hide out until their father returned for them?

Jessie's eyes lit up at the prospect of it all. Then again, would her grandfather remain lucid long enough to help them find their way there? Jessie had always been skilled with directions, but she had only been nine at the time. Would she remember her way now?

Firmly believing this to be an answer from God, especially, considering the miracle of the way the answer came, Jessie set her mind to bringing it to pass. First, however, she must tell the others the good news about Grandpa.

Everyone was overjoyed with the return of Grandpa's mental state. It was a true mystery! Sarah, the well-read one in the family, conjectured that the blow of his wife's death had triggered his former mental confusion. Now perhaps the second blow of his daughter's death had somehow triggered this restored mental state. Whatever the reason, the children were all delighted and while Grandpa, with Josh's help entertained the little ones, Jessie called a family meeting. Sarah and Micah had been made aware of their mother's request that the family stay together, but not that they were to leave their home, if necessary.

Micah gulped when Jessie said that they must leave, but immediately afterward he saw the wisdom in this decision. He had already noticed the way that Sean was looking at his sisters, and he had determined at any cost that he would protect them. Realizing that he was only thirteen, however, he had realistically assessed that he might not be much protection, but he would die trying, if need be.

Sarah was not so sure. She had signed wildly that they must wait there for their dad. Surely he would come soon. The Peace

Treaty had been signed with North Vietnam more than two months ago. If their dad had been captured, he would have surely been released by now and be making his way home. Therefore, Sarah opted to wait.

The deciding vote was left to Jessie. She, too, had noticed the way that Sean looked at Sarah and herself. Protecting herself was not an issue with Jessie. She felt capable of doing that where Sean was concerned, but she was infinitely worried about Sarah. What if Sean found an unguarded moment alone with Sarah? She would not even be able to scream much less ward him off.

Then there was Sean's attitude with the other children. Jessie wanted them brought up in the kind of love her mom and dad had showered upon them all. She did not want them subject to Sean's outbursts. There was also the issue of their grandpa. Jessie did not believe that Sean would suffer his presence much longer, even if Grandpa's mind was normal again. She feared greatly that Sean would have him put in a home or worse yet, even committed, and there would be nothing that she could do about it.

No, her mind was made up. They must leave and quickly.

Jessie's father had given her an old car when she had turned sixteen. By squeezing five younger kids in the back seat, Grandpa, Sarah and the baby would fit in the front with Jessie driving.

Sarah was put in charge of packing clothes for everyone. Each child would be allowed to take one toy or prized possession provided it would fit. Micah was to pack their camping gear. Jessie would pack their provisions, plan their route, and hide her parents' heirlooms. She knew that once they departed Sean would sell what was valuable. A number of items had already turned up missing, and Jessie suspected Sean of the thefts.

"When will we leave?" Sarah signed.

Jessie realized that she did not know the answer. They would just have to look for an opportunity. They certainly did not want Sean to know, so they agreed to keep things quiet. Jessie wanted all their things made ready for the moment when opportunity presented itself. The younger children would be kept in the dark about leaving, since they were too young to keep quiet around Sean.

Their plans were laid, albeit sketchily. Secretly they began to prepare.

Chapter Three

Sean had been leaving lately only to return with the smell of beer on his breath. Though, Sean still called Grandpa a crazy old man, Grandpa tried repeatedly to reason with him. One day Sean got so mad he almost hit the older man. Grandpa stared into his eyes unflinchingly and Sean backed off, shouting obscenities as he left the room and kicking at Ryler in rage as he passed the little boy. It was a close call that left Jessie shaken.

That evening, however, Jessie realized the time had come. She had decided to check the baby. As she softly opened the door, she discovered Sean pressing Sarah up against the wall! In a drunken stupor, he was trying to kiss her. Sarah was trying to scream with all her might and wrest herself from his grasp.

Jessie grabbed one of her mother's heavy brass bookends from the shelf beside the door and slammed it down hard on Sean's skull. Sean crumpled backwards, his jacket swishing behind him as he fell heavily on Jessie's side, knocking her to the floor.

Sarah collapsed in tears and crawled to Jessie while Micah, hearing the commotion, came running down the hallway. Upon hearing what had happened, he kicked the prostrate Sean, hitting him squarely on the shoulder. Then he dropped to his knees and hugged both sisters.

By now Josh and Grandpa had reached the door. "Jessie, what hap...." Grandpa started to ask and then turned to Josh, gently grabbing the young boy's shoulder to turn him around. "Josh, please go take care of the little ones," he directed in a soft voice.

Josh looked back over his shoulder at his Grandpa, uncertainty written on his young face. He saw his grandpa, however, place his finger up to his lips and quietly whisper, "Mums, the word."

Josh left obediently to do his grandpa's bidding. Though, his face had blanched at the sight of his uncle lying on the floor he obeyed his grandpa and did his part. He would remain outside with the other children and not let them know.

Grandpa stepped into the room and knelt beside Sean. He felt for a pulse. Sarah was hysterical. Jessie grabbed her by the shoulders and locked eyes with her, "You've got to pull yourself together! We're leaving tonight. I gassed the car up today. Now is the time." Then with compassion she added, "Sarah, I'm sorry for what happened. He didn't hurt you, did he?" Sarah shook her head vehemently, "No".

"Then, please get the baby and her things and go to our room and calm down. When Micah and I finish stowing everything in the trunk, we'll come get you. And Sarah, a good cry wouldn't hurt you."

Taking a long look at her parents' bedroom, Sarah clasped the baby close to her chest and slipped from the room.

"Micah, go get some rope," Grandpa directed. "We'll need to tie Sean; in the event he comes to anytime soon."

Jessie began straightening Sean's legs and arms in preparation for tying them.

She felt detached from herself as she worked. She knew that Sean would be in a murderous mood when he came to and she wanted her family as far away as possible before that time.

Jessie busied herself with straightening Sean's jacket while Grandpa checked the condition of Sean's head. As Jessie worked, a folded envelope fell from Sean's pocket. A Social

Services address caught her eye. Jessie carefully unfolded it. Her hand suppressed a cry.

Micah had quietly entered the room. Seeing his sister's distress, he dropped down behind her and read the contents of the letter.

Their uncle had given custody of Annie to the authorities who were to take possession of her tomorrow afternoon! They had already found potential adoptive parents for her, pending final news of the death of their dad. Social Services was also in the process of talking to a couple interested in adopting one of the twins.

Her anger growing, Jessie handed the letter to Micah and began to search Sean's other pockets. What she found there caused her to grow cold with fear. There was another letter from Social Services in response to Sean's request that homes be found for all of the children except Jessie and Sarah. The letter congratulated him on his upcoming marriage and stated that it was understandable that a new wife should have input on the number of children for whom they would provide a home. Understandably his attachment would be to the children he had known the longest.

Since teenagers were hard to place anyway, they thought that all was working for the best. Micah and Josh would probably be relegated to foster homes, together if possible but probably separate. As far as Sean's dad was concerned, they understood his need for care. Arrangements were being made to pick him up by the end of the week.

Jessie felt weak with relief that Sean had attacked Sarah. Without this happening, she would have had no way of knowing about what was to come until it was too late. As far as Sean's upcoming marriage was concerned, Jessie knew this was a ruse just to get what he wanted. She felt sick to the pit of her being.

When Jessie relayed what was in the other letter, Micah said, "Come on, Jessie, let's get out of here. We've got to do what

Mom said. We've got to stay together! I don't care what they think, Dad is not dead!"

Jessie tried to pull herself together to face her little brothers and sisters. Grandpa grasped her by the shoulders and gave her a fierce hug, "Jessie, you did what you had to do. I think he may have a mild concussion but he'll be all right. Now would be a good time to leave."

Micah and Jessie took one last look at their parents' bedroom. Then Jessie quickly removed from the dresser the photos of their mom and dad in their dual frame. Stuffing it under her arm, she reached her free hand inside the workings of the antique wall clock and removed a wad of bills. Her mom had kept emergency cash there. Now they were facing the biggest emergency of their life together as a family. She turned and walked out the door.

Micah locked it behind them.

Instructing the children to get their favorite small toy, they were told they were going to take a ride. They became excited at the prospect.

Grandpa was another story. He seemed so dejected that Jessie thought for a moment he had slipped back into his former state of not knowing any of them. Then he moved docilely to pick up his hat and his smoothly polished wooden stick, which he used for a cane. Grandpa headed for the door, without once looking back.

Suddenly Micah disappeared. A few minutes later, he reappeared with his collapsible fishing rod and tackle box, "This may come in handy where we're going. I can stuff the rod under the seat and I can put the box under my feet."

Jessie nodded. She wished they could be more prepared for the future but the trunk was only so big. It grieved her to leave her mother's prize possessions, but then, on second thought, her mother's prize possessions were going to be sleeping in the car with her soon.

With as little sound as possible, Jessie closed the car doors and started the engine.

Chapter Four

Jessie awoke with a start. Her eyes felt swollen shut and she had a terrible crick in her neck and shoulders. Dawn was slowly creeping across the sky as she turned her watch until she could make out the time. She had slept for two hours. At least that was something.

Then Jessie realized what had awakened her. The baby was making gurgling sounds as she took her bottle. Puzzled, Jessie turned slightly and signed to Sarah, in order not to awaken the others. Had she given the baby a cold bottle?

Sarah smiled from ear to ear. She had awakened soon after Jessie had fallen into an exhausted sleep, and prepared the formula. Then she had covered the nipple with a clean napkin and placed the cold bottle inside of her coat and the warmth of her body had heated the formula. She was very proud of herself for finding a solution to this problem.

Jessie breathed a sigh of relief. Not all of their problems would be handled so easily, but she was infinitely glad that this one had been. Until she had safely hidden her family, she was praying that the baby would be quiet.

Craning her neck, she looked into the back seat. Several blankets covered the sleeping children. She was relieved to see that Micah had fallen asleep, too, the red hair of his little sister sticking out of the blanket at his neck, where he had cradled her in his arms.

Grandpa was snoring ever so slightly and Jessie was glad for his rest. The baby was no worse for the wear, but even in the early morning light, Jessie could see the dark smudges under Sarah's eyes.

Driving for over five hours, her body tense the whole way, Jessie felt almost too stiff to move. She lay there planning their next move, thankful that she had found the remote campground that she had been seeking. She could have cried with relief this morning when she had finally seen the sign. Micah had stayed awake the whole time and had helped her look for it and it was he who had seen it first. They had made good time, arriving just before 3:30 a.m.

The next task was to feed the children and Grandpa when they awakened. Sarah had grabbed last night's left-over bis-cuits after she had pulled herself together sufficiently to face the children. She had suggested the biscuits for breakfast this morning with some of their mother's homemade strawberry preserves. That would keep them for a while until they could cook something later. She had also brought six hard-boiled eggs that she had planned to put into potato salad. It may be a while now until they had potato salad again, but the boiled eggs would give them nourishment this morning.

The brilliant color streaking across the sky was so soothing to Jessie's tired eyes. If there were not so many trials facing her today she would have thoroughly enjoyed the display of day breaking. As it was, she prayed and praised her God as she watched Him unfold a new day.

It had been Jessie's habit for years to begin each day with prayer to her Maker. This day was no different. Only, today her prayers were full, not only of petitions for the safety and welfare of her family, but that she might be able to find her way and quickly as she sought to hide them. She prayed, too, for Grandpa's memory. Remembering the campground had not been much of a problem. Remembering the trail to her uncle's property could be a trial.

The twins began to stir in the back seat, so their big sister knew that it would not be long until they would awaken everyone. Jessie prepared herself to be upbeat for the younger children. She would conceal her fears as best as she could...then she stopped herself in mid-thought. Would it not be better to just hand her fears over to the Lord and let Him deal with them, than to waste precious energy trying to conceal them?

Jessie did not realize it at the moment, but God was in the process of growing her up spiritually. Indeed, giving her fears into the Lord's care was tantamount to walking by faith. She would remember this moment later, but right now she did not realize the significance of it.

The next question was one of where to relieve themselves. Unless things had changed, this was still a primitive campground. Jessie unfolded herself from her cramped position under the wheel and climbed out into the fresh, cool air. Although, it was the last week in March it was still a bit on the cool side in the mountains.

It was invigorating even to a bone-tired teenager, as Jessie stretched herself into awakening fully. She looked around for the privacy of a bush and retrieving her mother's small collapsible camp shovel from under the front seat, she began to prepare a latrine. Suddenly, Josh appeared at her side with two tousled little boys in tow and said, "Here, Jessie, let me do that. These guys are in a hurry."

Jessie gladly turned that responsibility over to her little brother and opened the trunk to find the biscuits and jam. She peered around the trunk at one point to find Grandpa trying to lift his stiff frame from the passenger's side. She rushed to steady him as his leg muscles were taking time to unwind.

Micah awoke startled and was deeply chagrined to find that he was the last to awaken. He climbed from the back seat and immediately asked what he could do.

"Just help the others wash up and we will have breakfast in a few minutes," he was told.

Sarah had gotten the baby back to sleep by this time and was spreading jam on the cold biscuits. She knew her brothers would be ravenous. After last night, she didn't think she could eat again, but the mountain air was working its wonder and she found her hunger growing as she breathed in the cool air and sliced more biscuits.

There was a massive tree trunk close by and the girls had spread their checkered tablecloth over it. It was serving quite well for a sort of table. Jessie knew that Grandpa was probably missing his morning coffee, but she did not intend to stay here long enough to build a fire. She offered him the milk that had kept cool in the trunk of the car, like all the rest were drinking. He accepted it gratefully.

Getting him aside, Jessie questioned her grandpa about their whereabouts in regard to his brother's property. "Grandpa, do you remember how to get to Uncle Charlie's from here?"

"Well, let's see. I know we turned right when we left the campground before. Being unmarked and all, though, I guess we will just have to look for it."

"Should we leave the kids and the car here and walk or should we try to find a place to hide the car on the side of the road?"

"Well, Jessie, the kids and the car are well situated here so why don't you and I just walk. I need to walk the kinks out anyway and I think the kids need to get rid of some of their energy, too. This would be a good place for them to run and play in safety."

"Okay, Grandpa, if you are sure you are up to it."

They explained to Sarah and Micah their plans and cautioning them to keep the children as quiet as possible, they headed out. They knew this area of Macon County was so remote that it was not heavily frequented at this hour of the morning and they would only be passed by those who might be going to work and pay no attention to early morning hikers.

As the stiffness began to leave Grandpa's legs, he found he was becoming invigorated by the morning air. He breathed deeply, inhaling the rich aroma of the pine forest. Suddenly, three large turkeys rushed across the road just up ahead and Grandpa exclaimed, "Lookey there!" He seemed delighted with the sight and Jessie noted that he did not even seem the least bit ruffled by their circumstances.

Straining her eyes for sight of the trail, Jessie was noting with dismay that nothing looked familiar. She forced herself not to think about the possibility that they might not be able to find her uncle. Past that point she did not know just what they would do. Grandpa stopped for a moment to lean on his cane and ponder their surroundings. "Well, now, Jessie. Things have growed up a might. We'll find it though. Just you wait and see."

He had seemed to sense her dismay and Jessie, not wanting to worry her grandpa, stated cheerily, "Of course we will! If anyone can find it, we can. Didn't I get my sense of direction from you? Mama always did say that I took after you on that score."

A shot of pain went through her heart at her mention of her mother. Was it possible that it had been almost two weeks and was it possible that they were in hiding, trying to fulfill her mother's dying request? It did not seem possible. Jessie would wake up any moment and find that it was all a bad dream. Depression clutched its roughened fingers at her mind and she fought to ward it off. She MUST stay focused. She HAD to for her mother and for them all.

After a while, even Grandpa conceded that they must have passed it. Jessie had not ceased praying. They must find the old logging road and soon, before they were discovered.

As they turned around and headed back the way they had come, Grandpa stopped, removed his hat and smoothing his gray hair asked, "Jessie, how long ago was it that we were here?"

"It was about seven years ago, Grandpa."

"Well, now, seven years is a long time and in these pine forests young saplings spring up overnight. 'Peers to me that we are going about this all wrong. We're a looking for a logging road the way it appeared seven years ago. What we NEED to be a looking for is a path of young saplings or young trees."

"What do you mean, Grandpa?" asked Jessie, her hopes growing slightly.

"Well, a rutty logging road would be a mighty good place to catch pine cones and water would stand in the ruts in rainy weather making a nice place to grow up some young saplings in a hurry. We need to be looking for some younger trees 'stead of a road."

Jessie immediately saw the veracity of his words and walked faster in her excitement and impatience.

They had walked about a half mile when they came upon a path of younger trees that wound its way into the dense forest. Jessie cut out immediately in the direction that they led and was soon swallowed up in the dim light. Grandpa waited just inside the forest.

Presently, Jessie returned with consternation on her face. "Grandpa, it appears that you are right. This was an old logging road and I came to the huge boulder on the left that I remember was one of our landmarks when we were here before... but it doesn't look like anyone has been through here in a long time...." Jessie's voice trailed off. She had never considered the possibility that Uncle Charlie might have moved or worse still that something might have happened to him.

Charlie and her grandpa had both been in love with the same woman, her grandmother. Therefore, Charlie had moved off and become a bit of a recluse after Kevin McAllister had won

Amy's hand. Charlie had not been in touch with them since their trip here before and had even refused to see her grandpa at that time. Jessie remembered her grandpa's dejected look as he had headed back down the trail that day at Charlie's demand that he vacate his premises.

Jessie's mother had looked so much like her grandmother that the sight of her had stopped Charlie in his tracks that day they had met. But Charlie was kindness itself to Kathleen McKaine. Jessie had known, at age nine, that there was nothing but goodness in him, and she knew that was why her grandpa had thought he might take them in.

Looking at her grandpa a long time, Jessie saw a torrent of emotions cross his face. She knew that he, too, was considering the possibility that something might have happened to his only brother.

Grandpa raised his head and watched the pine boughs move softly as the wind whistled through them. He raised his hand to his chin as if he were considering their situation for the first time. He followed the dark trunk of one of the large pines until his eyes rested on the base and then he said softly, "Jessie, go get the kids. Bring what you can carry for our lunch and let's have a picnic up on Castleknob. 'Peers to me, the best we can do at this point is see for ourselves. I'll be moseying on up the trail. Take the fork to the left at the big boulder you described and I'll wait for you at the next fork."

"Are you sure you'll be all right by yourself, Grandpa?" Jessie asked with some trepidation in her heart about leaving him alone in the woods.

"Yes, Child. You just concentrate on getting the kids up the mountain. I'll wait for you where I said." With that he turned, seemingly lost in thought and with head bowed began trudging up what had been the old logging road.

Fearing that their car would be seen on the road, Jessie laded the kids down with their knapsacks in the campground, and the hike to what she hoped was their new life got under way from there.

They kept just inside the woods until she saw what had been the old road on the opposite side of the main road. Then furtively, in small groups of two or three, the family made their way across the main road, and were quickly swallowed up in the dark forest. Moments later an old truck passed where they had been, but the forest kept their secret as it would for years to come.

Chapter Five

The twins were in high spirits. They played with all their might during the day, but at night they continued to cry themselves to sleep wanting their mother. Last night, however, was the first that they had not cried and Jessie hoped for their sakes that this wound would heal quickly for them. The others, she knew, would miss their mother and ache for her for a long time to come.

This day, however, the twins used their excessive energy to climb over the tree trunks in their path and march like little Indians. They ran ahead of the others and hid behind trees to jump out moments later and whisper loudly, "Boo." Jessie had cautioned them to be quiet and maybe they would get to see the turkeys that she and Grandpa had seen earlier. They were trying their utmost to do this and mind their sister, Jessie, like their mama had asked.

The hike through the woods was so exciting for them. They had never been on one of the family's many camping trips. Their father had been gone for the last seven months of their lives and they had been too small before that. This was all new to them and they were delighting in the huge trees, the bogs filled with the first spring greenery pushing up through the fallen leaves, the birdsong and just the adventure of it all.

Josh kept tabs on the twins at all times. They were his special responsibility now, he knew, and he intended to do his job well. He, also, had excess energy today. He was able to sleep anywhere and he had rested well last night, even with the double dose of kicking that he received from the twins.

Micah was a different story. The kick to his uncle, which he had delivered last night in his frustration, was bothering him immensely. He had wondered all night if his uncle was all right. He had prayed for him throughout the night and had asked God to forgive both him and his uncle for their actions. With the little sleep that he had gotten, he felt very depleted, but he was determined to be there for Jessie. He would spend himself for her and all the rest of the family if need be. He had tried so hard last night to stay awake and watch over them all until morning but his eyelids had become so heavy after they stopped that the next thing he knew, Jessie was helping Grandpa out of the car and it was morning.

Poor Jessie, she had the responsibility of the whole family. She had driven for five hours on mostly winding roads and even then was up and stirring before them all, seeing to their needs. He vowed to do better by her and fulfill his promise to their mother. Even so, his legs felt like lead and he was fiercely hungry. His two biscuits with jam and a half-boiled egg had disappeared a long time ago. He hoisted his burden to his other shoulder, however, and with dogged determination, pressed on, bringing up the rear.

Sarah, meanwhile, though the baby was lightweight was showing signs of the stress-filled night. Granted she had slept fitfully, but her dreams had been filled with pursuers. She kept looking over her shoulder expecting to see Sean at any moment. Sarah had always gracefully accepted her inability to speak, but when Sean had grabbed her and pressed her against the wall, she had realized for the first time just how vulnerable her disability had made her.

How she had struggled to get sound out and though she had told no one, her throat hurt today from the strain of the effort. She had cried hot tears of anger and frustration last night and now she struggled to keep the flow stemmed. Jessie did not need any more burdens added to the already heavy load that she was bearing and Sarah willed herself to be strong, but inside she knew she was on the verge of collapse and it was aggravated by the suspicion that their father would never find them here.

She knew Jessie believed otherwise, but Sarah was missing her father and the protection he provided so badly that she did not want to wait even a moment more than was necessary to be able to see him again. Now he would have at least five more hours travel time, plus the time to hike to Uncle Charlie's, added to the time he could possibly see them and that if he figured out immediately where they had gone!

Jessie, on the other hand, had great faith in her father's abilities. He was a survivalist and had, on their many camping trips, taught his older children some of the skills necessary for survival. She KNEW he would figure out immediately where they had gone. Even while she was thinking this, however, she remembered that her father was going to be faced with the fact that his wife had passed away in his absence. He would reel from the blow of that, but surely concern for his family would serve to sharpen his senses and overcome the dulling force of his grief. Jessie fervently hoped so.

Jessie, in the lead, turned to check on the progress of the others and noted her oldest sister's sagging step. They had been hiking for about an hour now and so far the way had been mostly a gentle incline leading through the woods. The trail had started to climb slightly more now, however, and Jessie knew that Sarah would not be able to take the truly steep climb ahead without some rest.

"Let's stop for a moment and rest a bit," she said as the others caught up with her. A small bell of alarm suddenly started going off in her abdomen as she drew near to Sarah and caught sight of the deepening shadows under her sister's eyes.

Sarah had always seemed fragile and, of course, her quietness had made her seem more so. Jessie knew from their talks that she was grieving so for her mother and yet she had stepped into the role of a surrogate mother to her baby sister, uncomplainingly. Last night's encounter with Sean, however, had seemed to tip the scales where her health was concerned and now Jessie feared she was balancing precariously on the edge of a collapse.

After her sister was seated, Jessie declared that she wanted to hold the baby. She knew that Sarah would not be going much farther if she had to carry anything else, so she determined to carry Annie for her. Now she just had to get the baby backpack and strap it to her front and she could fulfill her mission.

With much protesting, after their rest, Jessie assumed the added burden of hiking the trail carrying her baby sister, as well as, her knapsack and duffle bag of blankets. Granted progress was slower, but for that Sarah was grateful. She was almost past going and they still had quite a hike ahead of them.

Jessie was growing apprehensive about Grandpa. Surely they would come upon the next fork soon. Just as Jessie was beginning to believe that one or the other party was lost, to her great relief she spotted her grandpa sitting on a tree trunk up ahead. She determined then and there that she was going to declare a nap time. Grandpa, too, was relieved to see his family. Upon seeing the circles under Sarah's eyes he also thought that a nap time was in order, so Jessie spread the blankets and the older adults stretched out. Josh was not the least bit tired so he agreed to watch the twins a short distance away.

Katy wanted to lie beside the baby, so Jessie snuggled down on the other side of the baby and moments later drifted off into a deep sleep. There was something about the mountain air and being in the quietness of the forest that caused all to receive the thing that they needed most—refreshing rest.

The sun chased the shadows across the faces of those sleeping and eventually the dappling effects reached through the subconscious level to awaken Jessie. Lazily bringing her arm up to shield her face, she lay for a moment trying to determine just where she was. The day felt so lazy and her body was so relaxed, the most it had been in so long that she could not remember. Then Jessie opened her eyes slowly, and squinting through the muted glare, she saw the pine boughs above her dancing to some unheard melody. Far above, the soft clouds scudded across the blue sky and Jessie felt that she could stay in this position forever—it was so peaceful and so relaxing.

Then she remembered. And reality came hurtling its painful way back into her being. She raised her head slowly and glanced around, relieved to see her sleeping family and also relieved to find that the crick in her neck seemed to be better. Her ears started picking up the hushed sounds of the forest now and the whispers of two little boys. Raising up on one elbow, she spied the twins still playing a short distance away with the ever watchful Josh. Her heart filled with love for her brothers and how they had played so quietly so that she and the others might rest.

She slowly inched her way from between the sleeping baby on one side and the still sleeping Sarah on the other. My, how refreshed she felt! She was up for the hike now and she prayed that the others had rested as well as she had.

Jessie quietly brushed at her wrinkled clothing and glanced at her watch. It was 10:30 already! They had slept for more than two hours! Well hidden in the forest they must all have felt that they could relax at last.

The twins suddenly spied their big sister through the branches and turned in mid-stride to fling their little bodies in her direction. Jessie grabbed them both up and whispered quickly that they must still be quiet until the others awakened.

Both boys tried to whisper at once about all that they had done. Josh had taken them on a short nature walk and had pointed out many new things to them. Now they felt that they must be experienced woodsmen and were anxious to show off their newfound knowledge. Josh stood proudly by, pleased at how excited they were at the way he had entertained them.

Jessie looked up at him between smiles and hugs and conveyed her thanks by the look in her eyes. Then Tyler astonished her by saying, "We taw a muntey!"

"A WHAT?" Jessie queried.

"A muntey!" Tyler exclaimed again but his brother interrupted with, "It was a mun-key."

"A monkey?" Jessie asked, looking back up to Josh for help.

Josh had thrown his head back and was chuckling softly, however.

Then he looked at Jessie and shook his head slowly, still chuckling. "It was a CHIP-monkey," he explained gleefully.

"Oh," Jessie laughed. "Well, I am glad you got to see a muntey boys, and I'm sure before our stay here is over that you will see a lot more animals that you have not seen before."

"Oh, boy!" both boys exclaimed at once and their enthusiasm served to awaken their grandpa, who looked in their direction quizzically.

The baby began to cry at that moment and Sarah was instantly awake. She, too, looked more rested and the circles under her eyes did not appear to be as dark. She raised up and reached for a squirming Annie as Katy opened her eyes sleepily.

"Can I help feed her, Sarah?" Katy asked softly.

Sarah, looking lovingly at her little sister, nodded that she could and the two prepared to feed the baby.

Once again, Micah was the last to awaken and this along with some other things served to put him in an ill mood. He still had a sleep deficit, in spite of this morning nap, but more than that he was hungry as a bear.

The twins, too, were voicing their hunger by this time and Jessie relented to fixing peanut butter crackers as a snack. She was amazed at how much of an appetite she had, as well. Since her mother's passing, she had hardly felt like eating and had primarily done so that she might have the strength to care for the others. Now, however, with the stimulating effect of the mountain air, her appetite had returned. She realized, with practicality, that this would mean more groceries would need to be bought soon. Even so, as she noted Sarah eating her third cracker, she was glad.

The family was soon repacked and heading up the mountain once more. Sarah had insisted on carrying Annie again, but Jessie determined to keep a close watch on her sister. The trail had become steeper now that they had veered off on the second fork.

They came around a bend in the trail and saw the stream that they had been hearing for the past several minutes. The stream rushed by to the left of the trail and the temperature dropped some due to the air-conditioning effect of the cold mountain water. It was both refreshing and invigorating. Jessie found her spirits lifting in spite of her concerns as she listened to the wonderful gurgling sounds and saw the beauty of God's creation. Also, the twins were excitedly pointing out everything they saw and their delight was infectious.

The family followed the trail which led by the rapids for at least twenty minutes. It was a special time for them and the water rushing by seemed to wash some of their anxieties and grief away. The splashing water clutched at the low-hanging rhododendron leaves and they looked like so many slim, green fingers dipping into the icy water only to bounce out dripping wet and then start the whole process over again.

The trail soon started to climb again and veered away from the rushing water as it turned to the right. Josh watched the twins closely and helped them up the steeper rock-faced places. He had not been quite two himself when the family had hiked here before, and he remembered nothing about the way or the mountains themselves. Micah, on the other hand, was remembering these same steep places and how his father had praised him for climbing even the steepest ones himself. He had been six at the time and well-remembered how grown-up he had felt.

Today, however, he kept Katy's soft little hand in his and helped her up those same steep places. The two of them had a special bond and he did not intend for her to even get a scraped knee from this trek.

Grandpa had to stop often to catch his breath, but he was strong for his age. A couple of weeks after his beloved Amy had died, his mind had started to go. It was as if it could not deal with the reality of the situation that his life partner was gone. His body, however, had remained strong and that was a blessing on this day, especially.

As Jessie climbed up the steep areas, she stopped to give her grandpa a hand where needed. His strength was amazing to her. She had thought of him for so long as feeble because he was so out of it. Now she marveled that he was able to make this hike at all, much less with the degree of strength that he was exhibiting.

She still wondered if he realized about the death of his only daughter. He had not mentioned her even once since the day of her passing. He did not seem to be grieving and Jessie wondered if he even remembered her at all or if he had lost remembrance of his wife and daughter both on the same day. It was a puzzle, but today Jessie had more pressing matters to occupy her mind.

They had been climbing now for an hour and Jessie felt it was time for a break. They had just climbed up onto a ledge of sorts. The overhanging rock jutted out sharply and formed a bit of a shelter. Only then, did Jessie realize just how blessed they were that it wasn't raining. Instead they had a beautiful March day. The sun had warmed things up nicely and though they were sweating from the exertion of the climb, it was truly a pleasant temperature, even without the March winds which were still blowing, albeit without much force.

Josh held tightly to the twins' hands, while Micah was doing the same with Katy. It was quite a drop off from here and both boys realized the danger that posed to the little ones.

They were all breathing deeply of the fresh, fragrant air. Even with their situation being what it was, they were enjoying the climb, the views, and most of all that they were together as a family. Each of them was deeply family-oriented and the older ones, knowing what was at stake, were thanking God in their own way for the fact of their togetherness.

Jessie knew that it was at least another thirty-minute climb to reach Castleknob. It was mostly uphill so she was eager to continue. The others stood, stretched and filed back into line for the last leg of the journey. The twins were tiring by this time so the thirty minutes stretched into an hour. It was really rough going and Grandpa had to stop often. Little Katy was becoming fretful, too, by now. She had passed her endurance level a long time back and Micah had resorted to carrying her up the steepest places. The rag doll that she carried, which was her most treasured possession, had gotten a smudge of dirt on its face and Katy was despondent about that.

Micah had tried to console her by telling her that they would all need a bath by that evening and she could wash her doll's face then, but Katy was too tired to be consoled. Micah himself was beginning to think that a hole had formed in the pit of his stomach. He had never been so hungry in all of his life.

Jessie was only too aware of the deteriorating morale of her troops, but she trudged on ahead knowing that the sight of Castleknob would lift their spirits once more. She dared not stop before that time for lunch, as she feared their pace would slacken afterwards and she needed all of the daylight hours that she could get in order to have her family situated before nightfall.

Grandpa must have been thinking the same thing because he was trying to keep them pressing on, as well. He encouraged the twins by saying, "Wait 'til you see Castleknob. It actually looks like a castle! Come on boys . . . let's get there before dark."

Jessie was now carrying the baby again and Josh was helping Sarah up the rough places since the twins had opted to walk with Grandpa to hear more about Castleknob. By now, Sarah was literally past going. The alarm in Jessie's stomach was ringing loudly now. What would they do if Sarah collapsed on this mountain? How would they ever get her down from here? But, Jessie continued the upward climb, praying even more fervently now, that her sisters would have the strength to make it.

Just as it seemed that they could not climb another step, Jessie pulled herself up over the last boulder and suddenly came out into the field that she remembered so well from her youth. There, in front of her, was Castleknob! Jessie's heart gave a clutch of excitement as she surveyed it. She hugged the baby close and then she called to the others excitedly, "We're here!"

Grabbing the twins' hands, Grandpa picked up his step and helped them over that last boulder, "Go see the Castle, boys!"

Micah and Josh both had to help Sarah up the boulder. She was definitely at the end of herself. Josh had climbed on up and given Sarah his all for this final climb up the boulder. Between Micah pushing and Josh pulling, Sarah finally attained the top.

Katy's eyes lit up with delight as she saw Castleknob and exclaimed, "Are we going to be staying there?"

They all laughed in their excitement and relief to finally have achieved their goal. Jessie was infinitely relieved and yet filled with consternation at sight of her oldest sister.

Everyone was exclaiming at once about the unusual stone mountain. They could see immediately how it had gotten its name. It did actually look like a castle, turrets and all. There were areas in relief which one could imagine were dark spooky windows. Smaller boulders stacked on larger boulders made one imagine the turrets and the whole of the mountain looked impregnable like the imposing facade of an actual castle. As the mountain rose, instead of continuing backward the stone came forward and jutted out at the top, making a seemingly unattainable stone ledge, such as the top of the wall that guards might use to walk along in a real castle. All Castleknob was lacking was a moat to give it that true castle feel.

There was a small waterfall which gushed out of an opening about midway up and on the right side. It turned into a wonderful brook which babbled along to the side of the field below the castle. The field looked ever so much like a huge, unkempt yard, with an obvious orchard at one end.

It was, indeed, a sight to behold! Memories flooded back into Jessie's mind of her first sight of Castleknob and the mysterious feeling it had left her with then. It was still imposing and she was filled with awe, once again, as she gazed at it, spellbound. She remembered how her mother had spread their tablecloth on a large flat stone and they had eaten their meal at this table. Her heart clutched with grief at the thought and she turned quickly from the others so that they would not see her tears.

The others, however, were too awed by the wondrous sight before them to notice. The twins ran around like wild Indians in their excitement and Katy clapped her hands with joy. Grandpa, though tired, had a huge grin splitting his face and Josh was jumping in his excitement.

Jessie turned Annie in her arms to give the baby a sight of the wonder and only Sarah was devoid of the excitement that the others felt. She stood with shoulders sagging and thought that their father would never find them here. To her, the mountain seemed formidable and in her present fatigue, it was overwhelming to think of her family living here on this mountain.

Suddenly, Micah exclaimed, "Are we ever going to have lunch?"

They all laughed once again at his obvious priorities and Josh yelled, "Hey, over here! It's like a big stone table! We can eat here!"

Jessie gulped and walked woodenly to where Josh stood and began doing what she knew she had to do. Preparations for their meal were soon underway with Sarah being given strict orders to lie on a blanket, watch the baby and rest.

As Jessie suspected it would, the sudden cessation of their hard climb, combined with the sight of the impressive Castleknob, and the knowledge that they would eat soon, boosted almost everyone's morale.

There was a small stream bubbling near their flat table and Josh helped the little ones to wash up while Jessie, Micah and Grandpa washed up and fixed their picnic.

Grandpa spread their tablecloth over the flat rock and Micah opened the cans of tuna fish. Meanwhile Jessie had scooped mayonnaise into one of their camp bowls and was dicing pickles into it. Soon she had a platter full of tuna fish sandwiches prepared and it was time to begin.

"I ont to say de bressing!" Tyler shouted and Jessie turned to look at him. Out of the corner of her eye, however, she saw her grandpa raising his head toward heaven and she said gently, "Tyler, you can ask the blessing the next time, but let's allow Grandpa to do the honor today."

She looked at her grandpa imploringly. It had been years since she had heard her grandpa pray and she somehow felt that this was a most important moment that needed dedicating.

Grandpa looked at her briefly and then said, "Let's all hold hands and I would be honored to speak to our Father in our behalf."

"Father...we thank you so much for your mercy on us today. You have protected us, strengthened us and brought us to this place. Now we ask, Lord, that Charlie would receive us and that we might live many happy years together serving you. We thank you, too, as always, for the provision of this food and for the hands that prepared it. Give us wisdom in the coming days and grace to fulfill your purpose. It is in the name of your most precious Son that we pray...." and they all said, "Amen."

The stack of sandwiches disappeared in no time flat, then the tin of homemade cookies was set out and also the bag of freshly washed apples. Even Micah was well satisfied with the fare and the hole in the bottom of his stomach was plugged up, at least for the moment.

Grandpa's legs were starting to stiffen so Micah offered to go with Jessie to try to find their uncle. Blankets were spread out once again, and all the little ones, including the now exhausted twins, and Sarah, lay down for a much needed nap. Josh and his grandpa kept a careful watch on their sleeping family as Jessie and Micah disappeared on up toward Castleknob.

"Jessie...do you remember where Uncle Charlie came from that day?" Micah asked, as he tossed his blond hair to the side.

"Believe it or not, Micah, I remember that day very well. We had all hiked up here just like we did today, only in less time. Remember, Daddy had stopped at the general store in Stekoah and asked the man who ran the place for directions to Uncle Charlie's."

"Grandpa had said that he lived at a place called Castleknob, but it had been a while since he had been there, so he thought it would be better to ask." Jessie stopped and turned around, surveying the view while she leaned on her newly acquired walking stick and caught her breath.

When they had both taken in the beauty of the sight, Jessie continued, "We all sat in the car and Daddy came back out a few minutes later with a bag of lollipops."

"I remember that! Mine was cherry flavored, my favorite, and we all rode away with white sticks sticking out of our mouths. I remember we looked around at one another and laughed out loud at the sight. Even Grandpa had one and Mother made Josh and me take ours out of our mouths until we stopped laughing, for fear we'd get choked." Micah gulped hard at the remembrance of his mother that day. It was a bittersweet memory.

"Anyway," Jessie hurried to continue, seeing the look on Micah's face and knowing what he was thinking, "we rode down to the old logging road, and strapped our packs on our backs, remember? Then we hiked up here and hollered for Uncle Charlie.

Grandpa climbed on up on Castleknob, like we're doing now. After some pleading, Mom had said I could go with him, if I held tightly to his hand and I was struggling to keep up with him when I saw a man step out from behind one of the boulders. He was leading a goat on a rope. Remember? He stood stock-still when he saw Grandpa and said in a perfectly level voice, 'Is Amy with you?' When Grandpa answered with a no, he said, 'Then get off my property.'"

Stopping once again in her strenuous climb, Jessie looked around, then continued, "Grandpa said, 'Listen, Charlie....' and Charlie said, 'I done all the listening I was going to, years ago.'"

"Grandpa persisted, however. 'Charlie, I want you to meet our daughter. I brought her with me.' At that point I stepped out from behind Grandpa to get a better view of Charlie since this was the first I had ever seen him."

"Charlie looked down at me and then back up to Grandpa. Grandpa quickly told him that I was his granddaughter and that his daughter was waiting below to meet him."

"Charlie looked me in the eyes for a long time and then he said, 'Like I said, Kevin, you are not welcome. I will go down and meet your daughter out of respect for Amy, but you can vacate my premises and I mean now.'"

"I felt so sorry for Grandpa as he bowed his head and said, 'I'm sorry you still feel this way, Charlie.' Then he turned, took me by the hand, once again, and we went back down to where Mama was waiting."

"Grandpa turned and looked once more at Charlie and then said 'Kathleen, this is your Uncle Charlie. You go on and visit with him now and I'll just start back to the car.' Mama gave him a puzzled look and then turned once more to Uncle Charlie who was looking at her as if he had seen a ghost."

"You know, Micah, Mama was always gracious and she walked toward Uncle Charlie all erect, like she did, and extended her hand. Uncle Charlie just stood there staring at it and then he took his hands and rubbed them up and down his pants legs and reached out one rough-looking hand to grab Mama's soft one. Then he clasped her hand in both of his, and said, 'Forgive me, but you look for the world like your Ma.'"

"Mama flushed and said she had been told that before and then she asked Uncle Charlie to join us for our picnic. Uncle Charlie's head jerked up and he yelled at Grandpa's back, 'Kevin, hadn't you better eat your grub 'fore you go?'"

"Grandpa turned and said, 'If you're sure....' and slowly walked back to join us. Grandpa introduced us all then and Uncle Charlie couldn't have been nicer. Daddy asked him where he lived and he said his cabin, 'Was in the purtiest place in the world.' Daddy said, 'Then it must be up here.' Uncle Charlie replied, 'Oh, it was.' But, he never invited us to see it, as you must remember."

"Then do you remember, he milked his goat for us and we had our first taste of fresh goat's milk. It was warm and bubbly and you and Josh drank until there wasn't any more! Do you remember that?"

"Yeah, now that you mention it, I do," Micah answered.

"Well, to answer your question, we are almost to where we met Uncle Charlie that day and that is the only clue that I have to where his cabin might be."

Both Jessie and Micah began calling their uncle at this point, praying that he would answer or simply walk out of the rocks as he had done before. As they kept turning as they called, not knowing the right direction and wanting to cover all the bases, they were both awed by the beauty of the view. It was literally stunning!

The brother and sister explored the rock formations as they called. There were many ledges and outcroppings and weather-beaten places that from a distance were what had resembled the windows. In places a few trees had taken root and appeared like so many bonsai plants in their stunted growth as they hung on to the side of the mountain.

The shadows were beginning to grow long when Jessie realized that Uncle Charlie either could not hear them or was not there. They would have to begin making preparations to spend the night in the open as it would be dark soon.

She and Micah reluctantly called off their search and began the descent down the face of Castleknob. They were close to the bottom when Micah, who was ahead, shouted in excitement!

"Jessie, come quick! I think I've found something!"

As fast as safety would permit, Jessie descended to where Micah was and then suddenly he disappeared!

"Micah!" Jessie screamed.

Moments later a chagrined face poked itself out of a rock face. "Sorry, Jessie, I didn't mean to frighten you, but come see! This may be a temporary solution to our problem."

At that the head disappeared again. Jessie, hurrying to the place, beheld a black hole in the face of the rock hidden in part by one of the bonsai-looking shrubs. A cave! Micah had found a cave!

Ducking her head, Jessie followed her brother into the darkened interior, lit now by Micah's flashlight. Micah was training the beam on the interior and moving it slowly around the cave, which turned out to be a nice-sized room at least ten feet high in places. There were ledges around the walls and Jessie, locating her flashlight at last in her backpack, trained it on the ceiling in careful scrutiny, looking for bats. To her great relief she found none. Then the thought of other creatures crossed her mind and she examined the edges of the floor quickly looking for snakes. Blessedly, she and Micah were the only two creatures in inhabitancy at the moment.

Then Micah trained his light on the center of the floor and discovered a small pit that someone had used for a fire. He threw his beam upward onto the ceiling again and followed a line of black to the opening. That must be the soot from the smoke, he theorized.

Other than the pit and the soot line, there were no other signs that anyone else had ever been here before them. Jessie walked over to her brother and hugged him excitedly, "Micah, you have found us a temporary home until we can find Uncle Charlie!"

Then both teenagers must have had the same thought, though Micah was the first to voice it, "You don't suppose that this was Uncle Charlie's home, do you?"

Jessie hesitated a full minute. She did not want to even consider the possibility. If that were true, then Uncle Charlie had not been here in quite a while. Forcing optimism into her voice, however, she said, "I don't think so, Micah. Remember he said he had a cabin."

"But suppose he just said that to Mom, so that she wouldn't know that he actually lived in a cave?"

Micah's question threatened to topple her hopes, but then her stubborn nature came to her rescue. "No, there is a cabin. I know it!"

"Well, anyway, we have a shelter for tonight," Micah stated encouragingly.

"Yes, thanks to you! I guess we had better go and tell the others." Jessie turned even as she was speaking, and headed back to get their family.

"I think I will go find us some wood for a fire," Micah said as he loped off in a different direction.

Chapter Six

Grandpa was greatly relieved when Jessie returned and told of Micah's find. Last night had not been so bad in the car, but the month of March in the mountains could be unpredictable and shelter was of prime importance, especially with the little ones. He closed his eyes in a silent prayer of thanks to his Maker, the One who had just supplied one of their greatest needs.

The twins were dancing around shouting, "De tabe. We onts ta see de tabe." Katy, too, joined in the celebration and marched to their cadence, hugging her rag doll as she went.

Sarah raised herself with some effort from her reclining position with the baby. Jessie noted with continuing alarm that her sister looked more drained than she had earlier. She must get some extended rest, and soon.

Jessie, herself, was energized from their find. She and Grandpa began the repacking process, once again, while Josh pranced with the marching party, keeping a close eye on their every move.

Moving closer to Jessie, Grandpa asked in a low tone, "Was there any sign of Charlie?"

"No, Grandpa...not yet, at least. We'll begin our search again early tomorrow morning."

Grandpa looked down, lost in deep thought, then he looked up with a brighter countenance and said, "God provided the cave. I am very grateful for that."

All was in readiness for the last little climb now, and Jessie headed out with her troops once again. She grasped Sarah's hand eagerly and said, "Come on, Sarah. I think you will like our new temporary home and I know you will love the view from its door!" Jessie was trying to be as optimistic as possible in an effort to raise Sarah's morale.

Katy, however, was the one who brought a smile to Sarah's face with her next comment, "Jessie, I've never stayed in a castle before . . . ."

Sarah looked up and smiled. It would be like staying in a room in a castle, sort of. She was still so tired, however, that her legs were trembling in spite of her effort at control. Jessie could feel the trembling through her hand and was determined that she would see that her sister rested just as soon as they got to their "room". Looking up as they climbed to their shelter, the family saw Micah returning with another load of sticks for a fire. Jessie was glad that he would be present for the family's first comments as they viewed his find.

Micah entered first and immediately began laying his armful of sticks on the fire that he had already started. Katy clung to Jessie's hand as she surveyed the dancing shadows on the walls. It looked like a painting come alive from one of her picture books. Jessie shown her light on the ceiling again to alleviate any fears that Sarah might have about bats, as Micah, his blond head bobbing, proudly showed off his find to the others. Then she unpacked a blanket and ordered Sarah to lie down, again, as she spread it on the soft dirt. Sarah had no argument left in her and still trembling, did as her sister commanded.

Shadows started to dance on the ceiling, as well, as Micah's fire grew with the added wood. Turning to his brother, he said, "Come on, Josh. You can help me lay in a supply of sticks before it gets too dark."

Josh, with a look of excitement, sprang up eagerly from where he was spreading out another blanket and followed his brother out into the late afternoon. Jessie handed them two empty plastic jugs as they went out, to be filled with the refreshing mountain spring water. The twins were instructed that running was not allowed in the cave as that kicked up too much dust, and Katy laid her rag doll down for another nap beside Sarah, then went to help Jessie in any way she could.

Getting preparations underway for dinner, Jessie realized that she would have to go off the mountain again tomorrow to bring up more food. What to do with the car was another problem with which Jessie was wrestling. She would just have to pray that one through until she heard clearly from God.

As Jessie prepared the baby another bottle, she realized, too, that their drinking water was almost gone. Not sure if she could trust the crystal clear mountain water, she hunted through the backpacks until she found a pot for boiling. Then she made a pot of coffee in their coffee boiler and the aroma filled the cave. Grandpa looked at her appreciatively and even Sarah expressed interest in a cup, hoping that it would invigorate her some.

The boys returned, loaded down with more wood that they had scavenged from fallen limbs, and they added some more to the fire. Then they began stacking a goodly supply up one wall. The room was bathed in the fire's warm hues now and the chill of the cave was dissipating. The boys, too, asked for coffee, and Jessie knew that the coals would form soon and be right for cooking so she began peeling off bacon strips and lining them up in the frying pan. Then she mixed up some pancake batter and let it set while she located the butter.

The water had boiled by now and she set it aside to cool. Then she placed the frying pan on their collapsible tripod and the smell of bacon frying was enough to rev up even Sarah's appetite. It felt warm and homey and cozy in the cave now, and Jessie was content with their first day in the mountains.

Soon the bacon and pancakes were stacked on the plates and Jessie quickly made some sugar syrup out of sugar and water and some Mapeleine that she had brought. Then she dashed it on the pancakes and Tyler asked the blessing, and the ravenous family ate their fill.

It wasn't long until the little ones, filled with their dinner, freshly scrubbed, and all tuckered out from their long day, were fast asleep next to Sarah. Grandpa, too, was nodding, but Jessie's mind was still too active to allow for sleep, yet. She moved softly to the mouth of the cave and stepped out into the chilly night air. A million stars winked at her overhead and she could hear her father's voice from years ago saying, "Look over there, Jessie. It's Perseus! See how the Milky Way trails through him." Her father was never more excited than when he was camping out looking up at the myriad of stars on a crystal clear night, pointing them out to his children.

This night, too, was crystal clear with the mountains clearly defined against the sky. It WAS breathtaking and Jessie delighted in the sight in spite of her growing responsibilities. Soon, she sensed a presence and turning, saw Micah's profile as he, too, was taking in the beauty of their surroundings.

"Micah, we have to find Uncle Charlie tomorrow, if he is here. We have to go back down the mountain and get the rest of our things, too. We'll have to take Josh with us and trust that Grandpa can handle the little ones himself. Sarah may still be too fatigued to help him. I'm praying about what to do with the car. We surely don't want it discovered," she continued.

"I've been thinking about that, too, Jess. It looks to me like you will have to sell it and probably to a chop-shop. I know Dad gave it to you and that's probably the last thing you want to do. . . ."

"We've got to honor Mama's request, though, Micah. The car is special to me, but staying together is far more important. You're just confirming what I already knew."

"Sorry, Jess."

"It's all right...there will be other cars someday but I only have one family," and saying that she reached around his shoulders and gave him a squeeze like she had seen her mother do so often.

Micah gulped hard and said, "I guess we'd better turn in. We are going to have a full day ahead of us tomorrow." With that, the two turned back into the hominess of the cave and soon had drifted into a restful slumber.

Chapter Seven

Blessedly, Micah awoke first. He was relieved that he had awakened early—and proud, too, of himself. He meant to be a man for this family, and he was going to have to fight his tendency to sleep late, tooth and nail.

By the time Jessie awakened, she was hearing the pop and crackle of a freshly built fire. Their dad had taught Jessie, Sarah, and Micah, years ago, to make camp coffee and Micah had just placed the coffee on to boil. The aroma awakened Grandpa but the others were still sleeping like logs, including, blessedly, the baby.

Grandpa suggested that Micah and Jessie might want to go ahead and look for Uncle Charlie. If he was up and about, which was likely at this hour, they might be able to see his wood smoke. Grandpa, in the meantime would get the rest of the bacon frying. The two headed on out and started the climb up to the top of Castleknob. They discovered that they were a little stiff and sore from their hike yesterday and this fact slowed them down a bit. It was necessary in their climb to scale the rock above where the water gushed out and formed the waterfall. The mist swirling into their faces was invigorating and they continued with renewed energy.

It was rough going, but they eventually attained the top of the end of the mountain closest to the ground level, which was the right side of the castle. They were met with a dazzling display as the sun was just topping the mountains to the east. The sky was a riot of color and Jessie's spirit soared within her at the beauty. They stood transfixed for a while as the sun continued its upward swing, changing the colors in the sky moment by moment.

They broke their gaze away, finally, as their stomachs began to protest, and scanned the horizon for smoke trails. They saw a steadily rising plume several miles away down lower in the valley, at what appeared to be a farm. Their spirits sank somewhat as they realized that nothing closer was visible.

Well, their day was set then. They would go back to the cave and breakfast, then hit the trail early to get the rest of the supplies. That way they could be back around lunch time or a little later.

The bacon was fried, more water had been boiled, and a stack of pancakes had already been eaten by the time they returned. The cave smelled wonderful as they ducked their heads to enter, and their ravenous appetites had returned as they prepared to break their fast.

Josh had taken the little ones to relieve themselves and was up, and only the baby and Sarah still slept. Jessie quickly outlined her plans to her Grandfather and he readily agreed to watch over the little ones in their absence. He meant for Sarah to sleep all day if that was what it would take to get her strength back.

Jessie carefully explained the baby's feeding schedule, and amounts, and about mixing the formula, though it was written on the box. She showed him where to find the fresh diapers, and first aid kit, and handed him her Bible, in the event he wanted to read.

They once again feasted on pancakes with homemade syrup and bacon. Jessie knew that the whole family could eat pancakes every day, and if she didn't get more supplies they would soon have to.

Setting out the items for lunch in the event that they were held up in some way and did not return in time, Jessie surveyed their new home. She did not think she had forgotten anything so she gave Grandpa and the little one's quick hugs, and telling the children to mind their grandpa, she made to leave. Glancing back one more time, she studied the still sleeping Sarah. In her heart she knew that sleep was the best thing for her right now. Sarah had worn herself out caring for the others since their mom's death and was in desperate need of rest.

Grandpa saw her studying her sister and said quietly, "Don't worry, Jessie, I'll see she gets her rest today, and I'll take care of everything here. Who knows, maybe Charlie will drop by for a visit." Grandpa tried for a little humor that somehow fell flat. "Anyway, you just take care of what you need to do today, and I'll see to things on the home front."

Giving a quick prayer that her grandpa would keep his lucidity, Jessie and her brothers ducked out the mouth of the cave and headed back down the mountain, empty backpacks and duffle bags strapped to their backs.

The wind had picked up considerably since this morning and suddenly Jessie remembered the old adage, "Red sky at night, sailors' delight. Red sky at morning, sailors take warning." She was filled with sudden consternation as she remembered the glorious display this morning and picked up her step accordingly.

The wind made talk virtually impossible, so the three filed down the trail silently. It was a huge contrast to the day before with the little ones chattering. They made good time, in spite of their sore muscles, and were to the rock overhang in seemingly no time flat. Stopping for a short break, they surveyed the clouds building in the distance and knew they would probably be in for it before the day was over.

They hurried on their way and only stopped once more to clean a scrape Josh had gotten on his hand when he slid down a rock-faced portion of the trail. Jessie had thought to bring a small amount of their antibiotic cream and a few Band-Aids. Most were used on Josh's scrape and Jessie was thankful that she had something with which to treat him.

They arrived back at the car in a little more than two hours. There were no signs that anyone had been there in their absence.

Opening the trunk, both boys started packing their back-packs as Jessie handed out their supplies. Within thirty minutes they were packed again. They were literally moving like lightning trying to outrun the coming storm.

Jessie had saved back another jar of peanut butter and a pack of crackers, and taking a plastic knife from the glove compartment, Jessie hurriedly spread the peanut butter on the crackers and they downed a quick snack. She knew they would need all their energy to make it back up the mountain.

Locking the car once again, the trio headed out to find the trail. The heavy backpacks and bags would slow their progress down considerably, they knew. Still they trudged on, bearing the supplies back up the mountain.

They were about twenty minutes from the rock overhang when the storm broke with a fury. The wind whipped Jessie's long blond hair, in spite of the fact that it was under her rain hood, and soon the sodden hair was lashing her face. Their backpacks, though waterproof, nevertheless, became heavier with the rain pounding down upon them. The wet duffle bags slapped their legs and their rain gear, which they had put on right before the deluge, stayed plastered to their fronts from the force of the wind.

The way became slippery and thus hazardous. They stopped more to help one another up the steep places, and Josh was at a definite disadvantage with his sore hand. He never complained, but Jessie had seen him wince a couple of times.

With heads bowed, the three tried to keep a steady pace. Their pants legs were soaked by this time, and water was streaming down into their hiking boots. They were beginning to feel really miserable and cold, but still they pressed on and, blessedly, they came to the rock overhang before long.

All three started shedding the heavy packs and scooted back to the deepest part of the overhang where it was nice and dry. Then Jessie thought of the towels in her pack and retrieved them, so that they could wipe their streaming faces. Out of breath and chilled, the three sat and shivered while their pounding hearts returned to normal. The lightning and thunder began in earnest now and it was truly a frightening experience.

Finally, Jessie, between gasps, said, "I am thankful this is happening today and not yesterday, and I'm thankful for this shelter, too."

Micah leaned his head back against the rock wall and tried to get his breathing to stabilize by drawing some deep breaths. "Yeah, I was just thinking that we should name this place Shelter Rock, as it certainly is a shelter for us right now."

"Great idea, Micah! Shelter Rock it is," Jessie enthused as her breathing became more normal. "This storm makes me even more thankful that you found that cave yesterday. Can you imagine the little ones out in this weather with no way to get warm?"

"You know, I was just thinking...we're certainly not going to be able to finish the hike in this weather right now, so why don't I take those sticks over there that are still dry and build us a little fire. We don't need to sit here chilled," Micah said.

"If you have energy left to move," Jessie breathed incredulously as she glanced at him, "then I am all for it." Jessie was far more stiff and sore than she was willing to let on.

Micah was true to his word, and soon a little fire pit was dug as his dad had taught him to do. He gathered the dry sticks and placed them just so, thinking of his dad and his careful instructions all the while. He stretched as far as he could around the perimeter of the overhang and retrieved some limbs, albeit wet, to place upon the little blaze. The wet wood was soon drying out and the warmth of a blaze was being whipped around in all directions by the wind, and the hiss and sizzle only added to the drama of the storm. The three stretched their cold, stiff fingers toward the fire's heat and when they were sufficiently warmed, removed their shoes and socks to reveal blanched-looking feet.

The heat was soon reflecting off of the rock walls and the three began peeling off their wet jeans. They each had one more set of clean clothes in the packs, and they unfolded the stiff and cold, but dry, jeans now, holding them to the fire to warm. When they were once again dressed and had on their dry socks, they positioned their wet shoes and sodden jeans and socks around the fire to dry them. Jessie was still rubbing her long, rain-darkened hair with the towel, trying to dry it as well.

Then they located the one blanket that they were carrying, and moving in close, spread it over the three of them. They were becoming less miserable by the moment, but were, also, hungrier. Jessie, glancing at her watch noted with dismay that it was already past noon. She hoped that Grandpa would not wait on them for lunch. She hoped, too, that he would not worry about them, as it might be a while before the storm let up and they could travel again.

"Well, boys, what do you want for lunch?" Jessie asked as she rummaged around in their pack refreshing her memory about what they had with them.

"Do we have any Vienna Sausages?" asked Josh.

"Yes, but how can you eat those things?" Jessie grinningly asked him. That was one food that had never been a favorite of hers!

"I'm going to roast them on a stick like hot dogs," Josh rejoined, "and have a hot lunch to warm up my insides."

Jessie looked at her little brother as if she had never heard of such, which she hadn't, and then she thought that sounded pretty good after all. Maybe she would try one.

She broke out the crackers and peanut butter once again. That would give them quick energy and, also, the Vienna Sausages and a pack of squashed-flat marshmallows. She also brought out the tiny folding can opener that her father had given her years ago that she always kept in her backpack in a tiny hand sewn pouch. Her dad always seemed to think of everything and she was so thankful for his provision and training now. She was hungry for pears and she produced a can of pear halves later, and soon they were once again full.

The storm showed no signs of abating and actually had grown even more violent. Jessie jumped out of her skin as lightning struck a tree not too far from their shelter and the earth shook as it thudded to the ground. She glanced at her brothers in alarm. Their eyes, too, were wide with the thoughts of just how close that had been. "If this continues," she thought, "We'll be stuck here for the night."

As if reading her mind, Micah chose that moment to comment, "We may be here for the long haul, Jessie. Did the others have enough food to last until tomorrow?"

"Well, it won't be what they might want to eat but they have enough to get by. There was oatmeal, more apples, and some fixings for a soup that I left for lunch today. I think they will be fine. We have the bulk of the food with us, however."

"Josh and I got in enough wood that it ought to last until tomorrow. At least, I hope it will. I would hate to think that Grandpa would run out before we returned."

"Maybe Uncle Charlie came by this morning before the storm broke and took them to his cabin," Josh enthused.

Micah and Jessie, almost as one, looked the other way. They both had given up on Uncle Charlie being on this mountain anymore. They did not know just what had happened, but they were, also, convinced that he was not here now. They were convinced that it was up to them to follow the Lord's leading in providing for their family.

Taking some dry clothes, Micah formed a pillow, and trying to make up for his sleep deficit, slept soundly while the storm continued to rage. Josh withdrew a paperback mystery from inside his shirt and settled back to read. Jessie, in the meantime, studied the roof of the overhang as she alternately prayed and planned.

Her thoughts, in spite of her efforts, strayed to her mother— and she found herself thinking back on that last day and how brave her mother had seemed in the face of death. She had seemed sad to leave them, but confident that God would provide for them. Jessie firmly believed that God was honoring her mother's faith even now.

Jessie had never been around death that much. She, of course, remembered her grandmother's passing, but she had not been present in the room when she died, so the actual act of dying had only been in her imagination until her mother's death. She had not wanted to be in the room when her mother died, thinking that it must be some horrible experience, which she greatly feared. But, actually, it had seemed easy. Her mother had just stopped breathing. She had made a supreme effort to turn her head slightly to see Jessie one more time. Jessie had quickly whispered, "I love you, Mom." And then her mother had just closed her eyes and died. She had made it look so easy, and Jessie had thought at the time that her mom had simply slipped through an unseen door.

She still existed, only in another state now and what a state it was according to the Bible. So, while Jessie missed her mother intensely, she was in awe, actually, at what had happened to her. Jessie had such a peace about her own death now and did not fear the actual happening anymore. Besides, her mother was on the other side to welcome her now when her time came. Jessie did not know quite how to express her peace to the others, but she knew that everything was going to be all right. She had lost her fear of death and she knew that God was in control of that. God was, indeed, growing her up spiritually, and she was relieved to let go of her fears.

Meanwhile, back at their shelter, a very worried Grandpa crouched at the mouth of the cave and surveyed the raging storm. He had prayed fervently that his grandchildren had been able to find shelter and had not been caught out on the trail in this.

It had been a worrisome day altogether. Sarah had not awakened yet and although she deeply needed her rest, he knew that she would be caring for the baby if she could. The baby, blessedly, had been very content today and had not cried yet. The twins and Katy had played quietly in a corner of the cave, Katy with her rag doll and the twins with the small trucks and cars that they had brought in their pockets. They had made roads in the fine dirt and were making hushed motor sounds as they careened their vehicles on make-believe journeys.

Grandpa had fed them their lunch and soon he knew they would be ready to nap. He eyed the wood supply appraisingly. He certainly couldn't leave the children to go fetch more. They would probably sleep through his being gone, but that was too risky for his blood. He knew how adventuresome the twins were already and he didn't dare leave them alone.

As the afternoon wore on, Grandpa knew that his older grandchildren were facing a night out alone on the mountain. They certainly could not travel in this and he prayed again that they had found a safe place to wait out the storm. He thought of the rock overhang and hoped against hope that they had been able to make it that far.

He knew his grandchildren were enterprising and that Jessie was mature beyond her years, but there were always dangers on a remote mountain like this. He questioned again the wisdom of coming here. He had awakened as if from a deep sleep to hear himself saying, "We could always go to Charlie's"—and then Jessie's arms had wrapped around him in a fierce hug. He felt he had come home at last only to flee. And here of all places! Charlie had ordered him off of this property once before. If he was still here, he could do it again.

But the children needed to be kept together until their father returned. He had understood that. Where else could they have gone to escape detection? It was so remote here with so many dangers, but the danger from Sean was a larger concern, he felt sure, than what they could face here, however.

Sean! What a heartbreak that boy had been! He and Amy had taken him in when the boy was only five. He was the only child of Amy's best friend, who had married a devilishly handsome man with an equally devilish temper and weakness for drink. The two combined to make a violent man who unleashed his frequent rages on his family. Sean had been abused since infancy and Kevin was sure this was at the root of his problem now. He simply had never dealt with or forgiven his real father.

Amy was sure that she could love the hurt out of the boy but she had given it her all only to be continually spurned for her efforts. Then Kathleen...Kevin stopped as if he needed to remember something important, but it was an elusive thought. Kathleen had been born and from that point on, Sean had been filled with a seething jealousy. It was like having the epitome of good and bad under one roof...Kathleen and Sean.

Well, they had done what they could for Sean and now all that was left was prayer, and Kevin believed mightily in the power of prayer!

Kevin suddenly stopped his wandering thoughts and returned to the present. Sarah was awakening. She looked around her in sleepy confusion and then her eyes stopped on her grandpa.

"Grandpa! What time is it?" Sarah signed in some confusion.

"Well, Child, it's three o'clock...."

"Three o'clock in the afternoon? I've slept all this time?" Sarah gesticulated her frustration wildly, but in the midst of it all, she suddenly realized just how refreshed she felt. She had just needed rest with no bad dreams and she had finally gotten it.

Suddenly she was pounced on from three sides by her younger siblings. "Sarah, you're awake!" Katy cried happily.

Sarah was given many sloppy kisses and hugs before she put them off and signed in consternation, "What about the baby?"

"Well, now, she'll be awake soon if you all keep this up." Grandpa rejoined jovially, but he was glad for the merriment and glad that the dark circles under Sarah's eyes were all but gone.

Sarah glanced around quickly to see Annie asleep over in the far corner. She breathed a sigh of relief and thought about how refreshed she felt. Then she gave a start and signed, "O my goodness, I must start supper!"

"Calm down, Sarah, and just you relax some more," Grandpa soothed, "We've already had soup for lunch and I reckon it will do for tonight as well. I'm surprised you didn't smell it."

"How could anyone smell anything while they were being covered with sloppy kisses?" Sarah laughingly signed her answer. Then she took a deep whiff of the simmering soup and did relax. It smelled wonderful.

Then concern creased Sarah's brow as she heard another boom of thunder. "Where are Jessie and the boys?" she signed. "Certainly not out in this!"

Grandpa took a moment to answer. "They are, indeed, out in this and I am hoping that they found shelter before it broke. I'm a mite concerned, but Jessie has a level head on her shoulders and I'm sure she thought of something to do." Grandpa had turned his head and stirred the soup as he said this, for fear that Sarah would see the real concern in his eyes.

Sarah sensed her grandpa's worry and sought to alleviate it, however. "Remember, Dad always taught us to carry our rain gear in the mountains, since the weather is so unpredictable. I'm sure they are hunkering down somewhere just waiting it out. They're OK, Grandpa," Sarah signed, after having clapped to gain his attention.

Smiling now, Grandpa stated, "You're right, Sarah, we don't need to worry. Besides, God is watching over them and protecting them, so let's both have faith."

The baby awoke just then and Sarah, while attempting to hand comb her long ash-blond hair, arose gracefully to see to its needs. Katy went along to help, and the twins climbed into their grandpa's lap and asked for a story.

"Well, let's see...." Grandpa said. "What kind of a story would you like to hear?"

"A 'towie 'bout tassels," Tyler enthused.

"Yeah, tell us 'bout dis tassel," Ryler cried, adding his vote to his brother's.

"Hmm," Grandpa stroked his stubbly chin and thought, "I could tell you about when Charlie and I were young men and first came to see Castleknob...."

"Yeah, tell us 'bout dat," both boys cried.

"Well, you see, Charlie was looking for a piece of land and happened to be talking to a friend of his about it, and he happened to own the farm next to this land. He told Charlie that it had just come up for sale and though it was rugged, it was 'beautiful beyond belief.' And when Charlie saw it, that is exactly what he thought, that it was truly beautiful beyond belief. He bought it right away as he had been saving for a while for just such a place, though he had no idea that it would be this beautiful or look so much like a castle."

"Charlie was wild with excitement about owning this mountain and promptly got me to go with him to see it. After a hard climb, we finally got to the top and Charlie whooped and hollered like a wild Indian. He kept talking about how he would be living in a castle and I corrected him by saying 'Don't you mean ON a castle.' But he just kept insisting that he meant to live IN this castle. That's how excited he was. He was beyond reasoning."

"Well, boys, me and Charlie spent the night in a little tent he had brought up, and promptly the next morning we made our coffee, and after another hard climb to the top, we drank it while we watched the sun come up. It was purty! Charlie got even more excited and...." Grandpa paused at his painful memories of how Charlie had told him then how he planned to marry Amy Garrett. Kevin McAllister had stood stock-still looking at his overjoyed brother. He had not known that Charlie was in love with Amy. He truly had not. He had been saving his own good news to tell after Charlie calmed down a bit from his. If he had not asked Amy for her hand only two days before, he would have walked out of the picture and left Charlie to carry out his desires. It had been necessary then to tell him about Amy's betrothal to himself. He would never forget the look in his brother's eyes or his bellowed admission that he had bought this mountain for her. Kevin had tried to reason with his brother, but Charlie would have none of it. He had left that day knowing that things would never be the same between them again. He had lived with that pain ever since, and Charlie had withdrawn from society, spending all his time on Castleknob.

Grandpa suddenly became aware of the twins pulling on his arms and rubbing his chin in an effort to bring him back to the present. He glanced over to see a very concerned look on Sarah's face. How long he had been musing he did not know, but he suddenly smiled and said, "Enough of castle stories for this day. I must tend to my soup."

The twins chorused, "Ah, Grandpa, jus' when it was gettin' good...." and trudged back off to play with their cars and trucks again.

Furtively, Sarah kept a watch on her grandpa. Surely, he would not lose touch with reality again. "Please, God, let him stay cognizant," she breathed.

The evening wore on and soup was served to part of the family, warm and cozy in their cave while the others ate cold pork and beans from a can and roasted more Vienna Sausages in their shelter on the face of the mountain. The wind had picked up and things would really have been cold and miserable had Micah not ventured out and scavenged some more wood from the tree that had been struck by lightning.

The rock walls, warmed by the fire, would retain their heat for a while and Micah had stacked the extra wood as a barrier against the wind. So, with the exception of a hot meal, the family members stranded out on the mountain were faring almost equally as well as those in the cave.

Chapter Eight

The next day broke over a freshly washed world. The wind had blown continuously throughout the night and dried the rock faces somewhat so that the trio could continue the last leg of their journey. They arrived at the cave just as breakfast was coming off the fire.

The smell of coffee boiling and oatmeal, with the rest of the apples cooked in, was overpowering to the three hungry hikers. Grandpa looked up as Jessie and the boys were entering the cave. He smiled broadly and said, "Well, I thought the smell of my cooking would bring you three running!"

The rest of the family looked up at his words and suddenly the morning was filled with squeals of delight as the young ones threw themselves at their brothers and sister. It was wonderful to be back in the hominess of the cave and with such a greeting!

After breakfasting on the creamy oatmeal, Jessie and Micah hiked again to see if perhaps they could find any trace of their uncle. They did this primarily to appease Grandpa and Sarah as they knew in their hearts that Charlie was no longer there.

Josh had been sent to replenish the supply of limbs for the fire. Blessedly, the supply they had left Grandpa had lasted while they were gone, but the last of those limbs had been placed on the fire this morning and Josh was given the job of finding more.

Upon Jessie and Micah's return to the cave, they discussed the problem of the car with their grandpa. He told them of a junk yard to which they could go in a neighboring town that would buy the car for parts. They would not get as much for it as selling outright, but, of course, that was not an option at this point.

They could buy two train tickets there, as well, and ride a goodly part of the way back by train. Of course, more supplies would have to be bought on this trip, so with Sarah's help they made out a shopping list.

By 9:00 a.m. the two were trudging back down the mountain. They made excellent time—and after stowing their empty back-packs in the trunk—they made off for the neighboring small town of Nantahala.

They found the junk yard, which was out in the country a ways, and began dealing with the proprietor. At Sarah's sugges-tion, Jessie's long hair had been pulled up and put under Micah's old fishing hat. Wearing Micah's flannel shirt and jacket, Jessie had assumed the stance of a teenage boy and apparently was pulling off her part well. The owner thought he was talking to two teenage boys.

A deal was struck and Jessie and Micah headed out walking back to town. Jessie was glad it was over but felt sick about sell-ing her first car to a junk yard. She focused on her responsibili-ties and fulfilling her mother's wish and trudged on, however.

Micah pointed out things along the way in an effort to try to get her mind off what she had been forced to do. Then he laughed and said, "You make a pretty good boy, Jessie. You didn't even have to change your name, either. Just think what would have happened if Mom had named you Susie! We couldn't have pulled it off then."

"You know, Micah, I've been thinking. Let's see if Nantahala has any thrift stores. I could buy some boy's clothes and keep this identity. That way if anyone comes looking for us here, it might throw them off the path."

"Great idea, Jessie! You and I are going to have to be doing a lot of hiking to get supplies, so that would be safer for you, as well. After all, you're kind of pretty for a girl...."

Jessie looked over and smiled her appreciation, then was lost in thought again, considering their next move. She was literally taking this one step at a time as she constantly tried to plan out their moves to ensure safety and provision for everyone.

When they finally reached Nantahala, they discovered they had just missed the train and would have to wait several more hours until the next departure.

"Let's go find out about a thrift shop while we wait," Micah suggested as the two made their way along the Nantahala River, which passed through the little town.

Finding a phone booth, the two pored over the entries until they found what they were seeking. It was only one block away on a back street so they headed out in the right direction.

The lady at the thrift store was most helpful, and soon they were laden with boy's clothes—a hat and sloppy jacket, and some extra clothes for the twins. As they were taking their purchases to the check-out counter, Jessie noted a section of used books. One was on identifying the local flora and fauna. It was lightweight and priced at ten cents, so Jessie added it to their selections.

Next, they went to the grocery store and stocked up with as much food as they could reasonably carry in their knapsacks. Then they made their way back to the depot with twenty minutes to spare. Jessie pulled out her new paperback book and began looking through it. Suddenly, she said, "Micah, do you know that vine, Kudzu, that you see climbing up and smothering the trees around here?"

"Yeah, what of it?"

"Well, parts of it are edible."

"If that's true Jess, that could help us out a lot. We surely can't be going up that mountain two and three times a week for groceries."

"I know. We'll have to see if there is any nearby."

The train roared into the station at that point, drowning out any further conversation, and soon the two were underway. Jessie was thankful that it was only March. That meant that the train was only partially filled and they had the economy open car to themselves so they could talk freely.

All along the railroad were places where the kudzu vines had climbed up the trees for the past number of years. The dead looking vines still hung in places with dried leaves. The train moved so slowly around the curves that you could almost reach out and touch the unsightly vines. Suddenly, Jessie turned to Micah excitedly and exclaimed, "I wonder if it would be possible to weave these vines into baskets. Maybe we could sell some to make money for groceries when our money gives out."

"It's possible, Jess. Sarah can make anything, so we'll have to ask her when we return."

The train was coming into their stop at Stekoah and Jessie and Micah disembarked as did other hikers with backpacks on their backs. The two made their way down the road in the direction of Castleknob. Soon, they were climbing the now familiar trail and Jessie marveled at the strength that was already forming in her legs.

Arriving back at the cave, Jessie's heart stopped in her throat as she entered to find Sarah and Katy in tears. Sarah was so distraught that it was difficult to make out what she was signing at first. Then Jessie did not want to believe it. It could not be true! Ryler and Tyler were missing!

Josh had gone to get some more wood and Grandpa had gone to get water, leaving Sarah in charge of the little ones. The twins and Katy had been quietly playing in the corner. The baby had needed changing and Katy had wanted to help.

While Sarah was occupied with the task, the twins apparently had quietly slipped off. Sarah had immediately gone to the mouth of the cave and had Katy calling for her brothers. The yells had brought Grandpa and Josh on the run, and they were out now looking for the two little ones.

It had been more than thirty minutes since Sarah had last seen them and it was only another hour until darkness would descend on the mountain. Fear for her little brothers almost threatened to paralyze Jessie. Then, too, Sarah was beside herself with guilt and Katy was crying softly, while Annie was screaming at the top of her lungs.

Jessie grabbed her sister in a quick hug and said, "This is not your fault, Sarah. It could have happened to any of us. Please pull yourself together. I am going on out to look for them. OK?"

Sarah nodded with stricken eyes. If anything happened to her brothers, she would never forgive herself.

Darkness descended with no sign of the twins. Grandpa and the others returned with failure written all over their features.

"Where could they have gone in so short a time?" Micah asked for all of them.

Josh walked over to where the boys had been playing earlier. He sat down wearily and leaned his back up against the rock wall, while the others discussed what could be done. He closed his eyes as twin tears coursed down his cheeks. Closing out the talking of the others, he was beating himself up on the inside as he realized he had broken his promise to care for the twins. He had wanted to get out on the mountain so badly and explore as he gathered their wood supply. Now look what had happened.

Gradually, through the background buzz of the others and his own relentless thoughts, there crept the knowledge that he was able to discern another sound. He must be wanting the twins back so badly that he was imagining their lively chatter. Then straining his ears to make it happen, he suddenly realized that this was real. He was hearing the twins! The noise was faint, but it was definitely his little brothers.

Josh jumped to his feet and looked behind him. Nothing was there but the rock wall. Then he moved around, straining to hear them better. This part of the cave had a little alcove where the twins and Katy had been playing. They had affectionately called it the little playroom.

Now Josh realized that the noise he was hearing was coming from there! But there was no one in the little alcove! How could this be?!

By now the others had noticed Josh's strange antics and a hush had fallen over them. In the sudden quietness, Josh distinctly heard one of the twins say, "Ee did too, say it!"

Like a mad person Josh leapt at the wall and saw a small opening behind a small boulder. Micah was by his side by this time and the two boys moved the boulder further away from the wall to expose a hole large enough for a man to crawl through.

Josh grabbed the flashlight that Grandpa extended and bent to crawl through the opening. He had not gone six feet when he saw his two little brothers making their way toward him, arguing to beat the band, and totally oblivious to the trauma that they had just caused.

Chapter Nine

There was quite a reunion when Josh backed out of the opening and the twins followed. The flashlight that they had taken was growing dim as they reentered the cave, so Jessie breathed a silent prayer of thanks that it had held out for them.

Grandpa sank down against the wall of the cave as the siblings grew wild in their excitement at seeing each other again. He well knew what could have happened if the boys had been lost on the mountain with night approaching. His relief at seeing them well and happy had caused his legs to grow suddenly weak.

Sarah could not hold the boys close enough. Her sobbing had turned to silent laughter at seeing her brothers again, so great was her joy. She quickly signed to them, "You must never leave me again without telling me where you are going! Understand!" Then her radiant smile returned and she hugged them even more.

Jessie finally found a moment to interrupt the reunion with the questions she had been longing to ask. "Boys, why did you wander off like that? Did you not know that Sarah and the rest of us would be worried? What if something had happened to you?" Her voice caught at that question and her mind flashed back, once again, to the day her mother died. She swallowed the lump in her throat and the boys, who had been standing with heads bowed at her questions, glanced up at her and Ryler said in defense, "Dessie, we onted to see de west o' de tassel."

"Yeah, Jessie, we foun' a hall an' onted to see t'other rooms!" Tyler exclaimed.

"Don't you know that people can get lost in caves?" Micah asked. "What if you had gone down the wrong way and not been able to find your way back."

The two little boys looked at each other. "We didn't see 'nother way," Tyler said logically.

"'Es, Mitah, we dint see 'nother way. An' we touldn't dit de do'r open, inyhow," Ryler added.

The others looked at each other, then Josh asked, "What door, Ryler?"

"'De big do'r!" Ryler replied as if everyone should know.

Josh looked at the others. Then he and Micah locked eyes.

"Let's go look," their eyes seemed to say.

Jessie spoke up quickly, "Boys, I would really rather you didn't go back in that tunnel. We've had enough excitement for one day!"

Then Micah looked at her with pleading eyes and said, "The twins got back all right. Surely Josh and I can do that, as well."

Jessie looked at Grandpa, "What do you think? Should they check it out?"

"Yes, Jessie, I do," Grandpa said quietly. "I trust the boys to use good judgement and I'd like to know what the twins are calling a door. We'll see if there is any danger, then we'll seal the hole back up, if need be."

Jessie still looked uncertain but she slowly nodded at her two older brothers, "Well, OK, but I'm coming with you. That way I can be sure you're all right."

Thus said, the boys scrambled through the entrance with their flashlights ready to explore this new find.

The passage curved back into the mountain and Jessie marveled at the lack of fear in the twins to come into this darkness. She offered a quick prayer that their fearlessness would not get them into real trouble one day.

Continuing to wind their way back into the mountain, the trio did not find any other passages that veered off from the one they were traveling. They continued on for twenty minutes or so and were just beginning to think that the boys had imagined a door when suddenly they rounded a corner and came face to face with a large WOODEN door! All three were startled to find this door so deep in the mountain. As they stared at one another wondering what this could mean, they became aware of a distant roaring, such as a waterfall makes.

Then Micah stepped forward and put his ear to the door. "It sounds like a waterfall just on the other side of this door!" he stated incredulously.

Then he cautiously tried the handle. It would not budge. He bent to inspect the hardware. It was a large brass fixture and, though it had a dull gleam, it looked ancient to the eyes of the young people.

"Do you think it's possible to get it open?" Jessie asked in a half-whisper.

"I don't know. I guess we could pick the lock. Maybe Grandpa would know how to do that." Micah answered.

Then Josh asked the obvious, "But what is a door doing in the middle of a mountain?"

Jessie and Micah just looked at each other. They were not sure, but they both thought of Uncle Charlie and wondered if he had put it there.

The trio returned to the cave to find anxious faces awaiting them. Sarah and Grandpa both heaved big sighs of relief. The twins had recounted their big adventure into the mountain in the absence of the three, then had promptly wanted to eat their supper. They were noisily scraping their camp bowls while Katy, who had joined them was sitting all erect, with her doll at her side, and spooning her soup in a more ladylike fashion.

"Well," Grandpa asked, "you three going to just stand there or are you going to tell us what you found?"

"There's a door there all right, Grandpa," Jessie exhaled as she still tried to calm herself from the earlier scare.

Taking advantage of her pause, Micah continued, with excitement lacing his voice, "It's a big wooden door with big antique-looking hardware. It's locked, too."

"Locked, huh?" Grandpa stroked his chin thoughtfully. "I wonder...."

"We were wondering if you know how to pick a lock, Grandpa?" Josh added.

"Well, that depends...."

"Also, we could hear what sounded like a waterfall on the other side!" Josh exclaimed.

"What do you think it means, Grandpa?" asked Jessie.

"Well, I don't rightly know. Some of these caves were used during the Civil War by our boys in Gray. Then, too, Indians hid out in them before the Trail of Tears. Blacks hid in some of them as part of the Underground Railroad, but I don't think any of them would have taken time to put in a door, certainly not the Indians, but that doesn't answer our question."

"What's the passageway like?" Grandpa queried.

"You have to stoop down and crawl through in the beginning, but then the roof gets higher pretty quickly and you can virtually stand the rest of the way," Jessie explained.

"How about other passageways? Anything veering off from the main one leading to the door?"

"No. It's simply a tunnel that takes you straight to the door— I mean, of course, that it winds its way back to the door," Jessie continued.

"Well, at least the twins weren't in any danger. That's a relief!"

"What say, Grandpa? Can you try to pick the lock?" Micah asked excitedly. All the talk of Civil War, Trail of Tears, and Underground Railroad had thoroughly aroused his curiosity.

"Well, boys, I spent all afternoon cooking you some soup. What say we eat our supper and think on it a bit?" Grandpa offered.

Disappointment was written on both boys' faces and Jessie giggled and said, "I've never seen you two postpone eating for anything that you didn't absolutely have to do!"

"Ah, Jess!" Josh exclaimed. "This is exciting!"

"Well, I think it's interesting, myself, but all of this hiking I've been doing lately, and the scare, has made me feel famished! Let's do eat."

So saying, the family gathered once again and thanked God for their meal, but most of all for the safety of the twins. Then they dished up the soup, whose aroma had become overpowering. They were hungry.

Discussion and conjecture ran high throughout the meal, with Sarah signing her questions, too. But no one really had an answer to the mystery.

After their meal, the boys wanted to go back into the tunnel immediately, but Grandpa's wisdom prevailed. He said that they had endured enough excitement for one day and, too, they had no way of knowing what they were getting into. They would tackle the mystery first thing the next morning with fresh energy.

The boys were very disappointed for a while, but then they talked into the night about what could possibly be on the other side of the door.

Jessie, who thought that she would be too keyed up from all the excitement and scare to be able to sleep, found that weariness was taking over. And she was to sleep the best that she had slept in over a month. Before she drifted off, however, she listened peacefully to the boys planning for tomorrow. She thought about how normal they sounded and how that maybe tonight, they would all go to sleep without weeping for their mother. Her thoughts then turned to Grandpa and how he was gradually assuming the headship of their family. She felt some of the burden lifting from her shoulders. As she had continually done, she fell asleep beseeching God for her family.

Chapter Ten

The next morning, bright and early, Micah and Josh were up gathering wood and hauling water. They cared for the young ones while the older girls fixed their breakfast. They had oatmeal with bananas cooked in and camp toast spread with peanut butter. It was all scrumptious or maybe everything just seemed better in their excitement.

Soon, Grandpa agreed that it was time and, once again, the boys crawled through the opening. Grandpa knelt and then lay prone for his crawl through. He had no trouble crawling in but standing up was another matter. The boys helped all they could in the narrow passage and finally they were on their way. Jessie crawled through last, leaving Sarah with the little ones, who had promised to be good. Jessie had wanted Sarah to take care of the little ones alone in order to help build back her confidence so the others were all going to check out the twins' find.

Excitement built as the foursome neared the door. Finally, Grandpa was surveying the situation as the boys trained their lights on the fixture. He did not say a word but a strange look had crossed his features. The boys waited somewhat impatiently for their grandfather to begin his work. To their amazement, however, he reached into his pocket and pulled out his own set of keys. He patiently laid the set in his left hand as he fingered the keys with his right.

The boys and Jessie looked at each other with concern. Had Grandpa slipped back in time once again? Then to their further amazement he selected an old key and carefully inserted it into the lock. He turned it but nothing seemed to happen. Then as Micah rolled his eyes at Jessie, Grandpa withdrew the key ever so slightly and turned it once more. This time they heard the ancient workings click.

Grandpa turned slightly to face his grandchildren who were looking at him incredulously. "This lock once belonged to MY grandpa. I could never bear to part with the key. It brought back a lot of memories..."

"Then this must mean...." began Jessie.

"Yes, the mystery of the door is solved. Charlie must have put it here for some reason. Now, let's see what that reason was."

So saying, Grandpa began to pull the door toward them on its huge, creaky old hinges. As Micah saw his grandpa struggling with the heavy door, he squeezed his body against the wall and together the two pulled and tugged. Both the frame and the door were made of heavy railroad crossties soaked in creosote, therefore, it took a lot of muscle to finally force it open. The sound of the waterfall grew much louder as the door gave way to the struggling duo, and the mist from it swirled into the opening, caressing their faces. A half-light crept into the passage and suddenly the door swung back to reveal the underside of a waterfall! The early morning light shining through the mist was dazzling.

Jessie caught her breath in wonder. One of the boys whistled and Grandpa had a huge grin splitting his face.

"Wow!" Josh exclaimed. "Who would have believed it?"

Grandpa cautioned them to watch their footing on the slippery rocks and they all moved forward as a unit. The view past the waterfall was incredible! It looked to the Southwest at multiple mountain ranges and over the morning haze that had settled in the valley. The freshness of the morning with the mist in their faces was a memorable experience.

Micah was the first to see it. "Charlie's cabin!" he cried.

They all turned to the left in the direction he was indicating and sure enough there it was! The cabin was somewhat silhouetted against the light and it looked like a picture.

"Well, I'll be...." Grandpa breathed.

They were all too stunned for a moment to move. They just stood and tried to take it all in.

Josh interrupted the moment by saying, "Let's go let him know he has company!"

Grandpa put out a restraining hand quickly and said, "Here, boy, you'd better let me . . . ."

He had taken in the fact already that no smoke was coming from the chimney. Kudzu vines, though in their dormant state now, had crept over the yard and had started up the far side of the house. Either Charlie had not been here in a year or more or else....

Grandpa did not even want to think about the "or else" but he knew this was something he needed to do alone. "You three just stay back here while I try the door. I'll signal you if you're needed."

Josh looked quizzical but Micah and Jessie understood. Jessie gulped and looked away as Grandpa made his way into the picturesque setting.

A tall fence surrounded the house and some of the grounds. It was in good condition from the waterfall side, but Micah noticed that it had succumbed to the kudzu on the far side. Grandpa was detained temporarily as he attempted to open the gate. The door of the cabin, Jessie noted, however, was not locked.

Five or six long minutes later they saw their grandfather stick his head out the door and signal them to come on in. The three moved forward, taking in as many details of the place as they could. The cabin had been built out of sturdy logs and shake shingles and seemed to be in fairly decent shape from their angle of approach.

They stepped up on the little porch and noted the old Kerosene lantern hanging by the door. There were two rockers strapped to the walls and flower boxes made out of logs stood on either side of the front steps. The view from the porch was stunning, and even with the overgrowth of the kudzu, it was evident that there was a barn not too far from the cabin, straight ahead off the right back end.

Grandpa beckoned them, once again, to come on in. They could not see the dim interior at first until their eyes had adjusted. Gradually, they became accustomed to the light and discovered a quaint little combination sitting room, kitchen, and dining room complete with a wood cookstove.

Jessie asked distractedly, "I wonder how he got that up here?"

"Hmm...." Grandpa said, as if she had called him back from another world. "Oh, the cookstove. I don't know unless it was a kit. Charlie was handy like that."

Most of the furniture, though covered with dust now, was handmade from stripped laurel limbs. Jessie noted with pleasure that her uncle had an eye for beauty and mentioned such to her grandfather.

"Oh, yes. Charlie was a craftsman in all that he did," Grandpa said with pride evident in his tone. Then he stopped in front of the mantle. Placed just so were old photos of his mother and father.

Turning about, he said, "These are your great-grandparents, kids."

The youngsters crowded together to see and Jessie threw her arm around her grandpa's waist. It was a special moment as the two generations stood surveying the third.

Josh once again broke the silence with, "I wonder if it works?" indicating with his head the old mantle clock.

Grandpa gazed at it and that nostalgic smile crossed his face once more. "That belonged to the doctor that delivered my poppa. When the old doctor died, Poppa approached his widow one day and asked if he could buy it. He had taken a shine to it through the years. She said she couldn't think of anyone nicer to have it...."

Jessie said softly, "I wish I had known him."

Then Josh voiced the obvious question that was on all of their minds, "I wonder what happened to Uncle Charlie?"

Grandpa was the first to speak, "I don't know, son. It's apparent that he's not been here in a while, though."

Then Grandpa said in a louder, more optimistic voice, "Listen, Josh, why don't you go back and get Sarah and the kids. I'm sure Sarah is wondering what's going on. When you return to the door at the end of the passage, though, stop and call. I don't want the twins to get excited and slip on the rocks."

Josh wheeled to do his grandpa's bidding and the others were left to discuss the situation in private.

"What do we do now, Grandpa?" Micah asked.

Grandpa glanced at Jessie. "What do you think, girl?"

Jessie hesitated only a moment, "Well, we don't know what's happened to Uncle Charlie, but we know he surely isn't here. Given the circumstances, do you think he would mind if we kind of moved in and lived here for a while?"

Grandpa lowered his head with a big sigh. "I know you both probably remember my encounter with Charlie seven years ago. If he ran me off then, the odds are he would do it again. But, I really don't think, once he heard the situation, that he would turn you kids out. Charlie had a big heart, after all."

Noting his grandpa's use of the past tense, Micah asked, "You do think Uncle Charlie is still alive, don't you?"

Jessie intervened, "Micah, I don't think there is any way any of us could know that for sure, but it does appear to me that God has provided us with a nice shelter. Wouldn't you agree, Grandpa?"

"It does look that way, child....I really don't think it would be wrong to clean the place up and stay here a while."

Jessie's eyes brightened at her grandpa's words. She just knew that Sarah would love this cabin and it would surely lift her sagging spirits.

Micah looked excitedly around. "If we all worked together, we could have the place cleaned up and be moved in by nightfall!"

"Slow down a bit, boy! There's more to be done here than a little dusting. We'll need to check the stove out thoroughly and make sure no varmints are living in it or the chimney either. Then we need to repair that fencing so that the twins can't get through it and wander off. Let's just proceed with caution. We'll get moved in at the proper time."

The three continued exploring and their excitement mounted. They discovered a spring house just outside the kitchen. Uncle Charlie had piped water straight from a spring that flowed out of the side of the mountain into the spring house. Then he had diverted a portion of the flow into another pipe that went straight into the kitchen. No more hauling water— they had gravity water!

Grandpa explained that the wood cookstove was equipped with a water reservoir which Uncle Charlie had also piped into the bathroom. They could all take hot baths soon!

Of special interest to Jessie was a fairly large pantry which still contained a store of foodstuffs. Uncle Charlie apparently had canned his own food and the shelves were lined with jars. Most were empty and some had obviously spoiled but there were a number that looked all right. There must have been fifteen or sixteen jars of peaches and pears that looked perfectly fine. Jessie imagined the peach cobblers that Sarah would make with them. Yum!

There was a smoke house not far away. It was locked up tight, but a small hole in the wood revealed that several hams still hung from the ceiling. Jessie did not like the smell and quickly turned away.

The hen house was in need of some minor repairs, but Grandpa was relieved to find no carcasses. If his brother had been injured on this mountain and died here, there should certainly be some indication of that, somewhere. He was getting more of the feeling that his brother might have grown tired of the seclusion and its inherent loneliness and simply moved elsewhere. Of course, the hams and the canned food might indicate otherwise. He just didn't know what to make of it.

The barn, though beginning to be covered with kudzu was sturdy and sound. Jessie entered its dark interior first, followed by Micah. Poking her head into a stall to check out its status, she suddenly screamed and fell backwards. Over her outstretched legs, something white streaked by. Micah turned at the scream, just in time to catch sight of a very frightened goat. It rounded the corner and almost plowed into Grandpa.

Just as Jessie was picking herself up, she heard a frightened bleat and fell once more as two kids ran past her. Micah made a mad dive as the kids approached him running helter-skelter. To his utter amazement, he caught one. It was a supreme effort to hold on to the wriggling, squirming being and just as he was losing the battle, he felt Grandpa's strong arms grasping the kid by its shoulders. He had it!

"Good work, boy!" Grandpa half-whispered breathlessly.

"Now, we'll contain this little one and its mom will surely come back when she hears its cries. Then we'll have fresh milk!"

"My thoughts, exactly!" Micah breathed from his prone position on the barn floor.

Jessie, who was still stunned from the encounters, came shakily into the light. Then she burst out laughing at sight of Micah. "Next time, you can go first!" she said in earnest.

Micah looked sheepishly up at her, then he raised himself slowly, brushing off debris as he did so. Jessie glanced at the frightened kid in Grandpa's arms. It had calmed down some as Grandpa whispered soothingly in its ear.

It wasn't very old and Jessie felt sorrow for it at being separated from its mother. Oh, well, if they could catch the nanny, then they would all benefit.

Grandpa and Micah immediately began to find the best place to keep the kid until its mother returned. Jessie, suddenly, didn't feel as bold in her exploring. She decided to watch from a distance. The kid, who was bleating furiously now, was penned and Micah climbed into the barn loft to see if there was a store of hay. Blessedly, there was and he brought down an armload to place in the stall with the frightened baby goat.

Grandpa found a storage room in the meantime and located a small can of oil. He began oiling the hinges on the barn door. They were stuck fast and his intent was to close these doors once the nanny goat came inside to check on her baby.

Jessie still reclined against a stump and gazed on the beauty of her surroundings. She was slowly but surely catching her breath. "What if it had been a bear!" she thought and shivered involuntarily.

Grandpa had the hinges working now and he and Micah rigged a way to close them quickly once the mother goat went inside. Then while they hid and waited, Jessie went back to the cabin and checked out the bedroom more closely.

There was one feather bed. The mattress had obviously been made by her uncle. Was there anything that he hadn't been able to do? There were oil lamps on either side of the bed sitting on handmade night stands. They were almost half full.

The chifferobe in the corner was still full of Uncle Charlie's clothes and shoes. Jessie wondered again what had happened to him.

There was a blanket chest against the other wall. It was lined with cedar and contained two blankets, two beautiful quilts and some personal papers of Uncle Charlie's which Jessie left untouched.

A washstand stood in the corner and a beautiful oval mirror hung above it. The bedroom window looked out on the water-fall and Jessie thought that one could surely sleep well on the mountain with the sound of that waterfall in the background.

Exploring further, Jessie discovered a rope hanging from the ceiling in the corner of the sitting room. She pulled on it gently and heard the boards overhead give. Tugging a little harder she found the rope pulled down a door in the ceiling and revealed a step ladder that when slid downward touched the floor. She decided to await the arrival of the others before exploring that find. Cautiously, she pushed the ladder back upwards and re-leased the catch so that the door could swing closed once again.

She was startled by a jubilant shout from Micah and ran to the back in time to witness grandfather and grandson slapping one another on the back and shaking hands victoriously. They had captured the nanny goat, apparently.

Jessie picked her way over the dead kudzu vines back to where they were standing. Success was written all over their faces and Micah shouted, "Hey, Jess, we'll have warm milk for the little ones tonight! And, don't worry, we caught the other little kid, too."

Relieved to hear that, Jessie came to stand with the jubilant duo. "That was pretty smart of you to think so quickly to catch that kid. I know I wasn't thinking along those lines."

"Well, you didn't even know what was coming at you! You probably thought it was a bear or something!"

Jessie blushed at that statement and ventured in her defense, "I really wasn't expecting to see a goat in a barn that I thought was empty! Grandpa, do you suppose that goat belonged to Uncle Charlie or was just wild on the mountain?"

"I couldn't say for sure, Jess, but I have a feeling that it knew Uncle Charlie. The stall, where you surprised it, has an open-ing up into the hayloft. Charlie probably threw hay down to it there. I'm just guessing, of course," Grandpa answered.

Looking toward the waterfall, Grandpa mused, "I would have thought that Sarah and the others would have been here by now. It must be close to 11:00."

"If they are not here in the next little bit I'll head back to check on them," Micah offered.

Jessie told of her find in the sitting room and the trio headed back to check it out. The ceiling door and ladder were pulled down once again and Micah ventured into the attic. "Hey, there's another bedroom up here with a cot and a bed that looks bigger than a twin," he shouted. "There are lots of cobwebs and a mouse nest or two but I think it will clean up just fine."

"Good!" Grandpa declared. "If the bed is an old white iron one, then that is the one that Charlie and I used when we were growing up. It's called a three-quarters bed. We can put all you boys up there. I will take the couch and the girls can have the bedroom...."

"No, Grandpa. You need to take the bedroom," Jessie interjected.

"Jess, there'll be no discussion. I appreciate you wanting to give me a nice soft bed, but you girls are going to take it and that's settled."

"All right, Grandpa, if that's the way you want it. Where can we put the baby, though?"

"Well, now...I have that all figured out. Just you come with me." And Grandpa motioned for her to follow.

He took her into the bedroom and went over to the chiffer-obe. There were four large deep drawers on the bottom, two to a side, and Grandpa pulled out one of the top ones. "When I was a boy, we always used a drawer as a crib when we were visiting relatives that didn't have kids or weren't prepared for them or simply had too many. It worked just fine back then and I reckon it will work fine now until we can get a cradle built."

Jessie agreed that solution would work temporarily. Grandpa declared that he would still have his privacy as he would be the last to go to bed and the first to arise, so sleeping arrangements had been settled.

They heard a whistle at that point and rushed out to see Josh wildly waving his arms. Sarah stood behind him, holding the baby and looking in awe and consternation at the waterfall. Katy clung to her skirt and Ryler and Tyler stood just in front where Sarah could keep an eye on them.

The others ran to help and discovered that Sarah had thought to pack a lunch. That was what had taken so long. Excitement ran high as everyone talked at once, telling the newcomers of their finds.

Sarah and the little ones were then given a quick tour. Her cheeks pink with excitement, Sarah signed finally that she could see more at a later time, but the little ones must be fed.

They all washed up at the kitchen sink in the freezing spring water. With benumbed fingers, the family stood for prayer as Grandpa thanked God for His provision. Then they tore into their lunch and discussed the marvel of their new home, while sitting on the front porch looking out at the magnificent view.

"I declare; I do believe Charlie was right!" Grandpa exclaimed at length. "His cabin is in the most beautiful spot in the world."

Sarah was enchanted with the place, the waterfall, the view, the quaintness of the cabin, the provision of some food, which they, of course, would replace in due time. They would be safe here from Sean. He would NEVER find them here. Then suddenly, it hit her. If Sean could not find them, then their dad would not be able to either!

Jessie noticed Sarah's sudden downcast look and guessing instinctively what she was thinking said, "Sarah, if you are thinking that Dad will never find us here, please don't worry. We will find some way to let him know. We will pray and God will direct us in this, just as He has directed our footsteps here. Just think, Sarah, if the twins had not wanted to see more of the 'tassel' we may never have known this was here. If God could work all that out, can't we trust Him to work everything else out as well?"

Sarah glanced up at her sister with the light of understanding dawning in her eyes. "Of course, He can!" she signed excitedly. "I have been so faithless, Jessie...can you ever forgive me?"

"What's there to forgive, Sarah?" Jessie smiled contentedly.

"No, Jessie, I mean it. You have tried so hard to be positive about all of this. You have been trying to walk by faith and I have been a stumbling block in your path. I see that so clearly now. Please forgive me. I intend to walk by faith, too, now!" Sarah's chin came up emphatically as she signed the last.

"OK, Sarah. If you insist, then I forgive you. We'll both walk by faith together and help each other through this."

"NOW, we can!" Sarah beamed.

"Listen," Jessie said, "do you want to keep the little ones while I clean or how do you want to do this?"

"Why don't we take turns? That way you won't be over-worked with the cleaning and you'll get to enjoy the kids some, too. You have been so busy taking care of everything for all of us that you haven't gotten to spend much time with them," Sarah signed.

"If that's how you would like to do things, Sarah, then it's done!" Jessie exclaimed enthusiastically.

Thus the major job of cleaning began. Sarah took the first shift and started in the pantry, going through and assessing the stock of food, while Grandpa and Micah started cleaning out the stove.

Josh's job was to pull the few kudzu vines off the side of the house. Jessie suggested that he stack the vines all together just inside the barn for use later in basket weaving. All went well, and Jessie thoroughly enjoyed the time she spent watching the younger children.

Sarah, in her job of cleaning, would look up occasionally and smile as she heard her sister's peals of laughter as she played with the kids. They were fulfilling their dying mother's request that they all stay together, and Sarah felt a sense of peace as she thought on that. Her mother would be pleased to see how it was all working out. Her mother would be pleased, too, that apparently the shock of her death had somehow seemed to restore her poppa's mind. If their dad could just see them now, too, he would be proud of the way that they were utilizing the things that he had taught them and how they were working together. Sarah felt a deep sense of satisfaction, even amidst her grief, as she thought on these things.

It took a while to clean the wood cookstove, stovepipe, and chimney, and to make sure it was safe to light a fire. Finally, however, Grandpa declared that they could try it. The first attempt indicated that the stove drew well, and as they all gathered around to witness the flames licking at the tender wood, Grandpa relayed some more of their history.

"You know, kids, your great-great grandmother, my grandmother, was a mid-wife who birthed all the area babies. When she wasn't birthing babies, however, she was in great demand as a chimney builder. It was said that no one could build a chimney that could draw any better than Sarah Ainsworth could. 'Peers to me that Charlie must have inherited her trait, building chimneys, that is."

They all laughed at the obvious joke. Somehow, their image of Uncle Charlie didn't lend itself to midwifery.

Uncle Charlie's piping of water to the cookstove was a blessing appreciated right away. Turning the valve, the newly cleaned reservoir was filled in no time. Soon there would be hot water for the rest of the chores.

Micah and Josh hit the attic bedroom next and soon the debris and nests were removed, the furniture dusted, floor swept and mopped, and the window panes at each end were sparkling clean, inside and out. The mattress was taken outside to be beaten and aired out, meanwhile Grandpa had been cleaning out the fireplace and checking it for draw as well. Josh then agreed to watch the young ones for a short time to allow the girls to work together in the kitchen.

Since the wood cookstove had been cleaned, the girls could move into the main living area with their cleaning. They managed to get the kitchen cleaning well underway before they had to knock off and head back to the cave to prepare dinner.

Jessie talked excitedly to Sarah's back as they headed back down the tunnel to the cave, with some tired little ones in tow. She was laying out their plans for the next day. Both girls felt sure that they could go ahead and move all of their belongings out of the cave the next morning. It was going to be so good to live in a house again, and such a neat one at that!

The little ones were laid down for a late afternoon nap while the girls quickly fell to preparing their evening meal. Josh had remained behind with Grandpa and Micah to do some more clearing of the kudzu.

"Let's get up early in the morning, Sarah, and watch our last sunrise together from this side of the mountain. It will be like we are truly saying goodbye to one segment of our lives and beginning a whole new era, won't it?" Jessie asked.

Sarah, with her ash-blond head bent over the meal she was preparing, looked a little nostalgic before signing her reply, "I think that would be nice. You know, Jessie, it is both exciting and scary. We will be virtually cut off from civilization."

"It will be different, that's for sure, but we will be together, Sarah. Together for Mama...."

The evening continued to run high with excitement and plans for their future. The story was retold of the discovery and ultimate capture of the nanny goat and her kids, amidst squeals of laughter, as the young ones enjoyed the fresh goat's milk. A milking stand had been located at the other end of the barn and the goat apparently had been milked before, as without too much difficulty, it had submitted to the milking.

Suddenly, everyone felt tired from their day's adventures and they all turned in early, in anticipation of the next day's move.

Chapter Eleven

Bright and early the next morning, the girls, as planned, arose and went to meet the new day. The sunrise was a glorious event, vividly coloring the fresh new day, and they once again reveled in the beauty of their surroundings. Just as they were turning to reenter the cave, however, Sarah grabbed Jessie's sleeve and signed quickly to look at the corner of the field.

Turning quietly, Jessie saw to her great joy, a doe step gracefully, though timidly, into the open field near the orchard, sniffing the air as she went. Behind her, twin fawns broke into the open and ran and chased each other. Two more does followed the three and began foraging through the dead grasses. Jessie held her breath with the wonder of it all.

Soon, the others were up and breakfast had been served. Grandpa and the older siblings took to packing, while Josh again watched the young ones. As much as could be carried was packed onto their backs and the family began their move through the mountain.

The tunnel rang with the chatter of the twins, and in no time at all the group emerged into the mist of the waterfall. The children were soon settled again on the porch to play and the older members fell to their individual tasks. Grandpa finished checking out the chimney of the fireplace then built a fire, while Jessie dreamed of the bath that she would surely have before this day was over.

They all pitched in to clean the living area, and by noon they had moved the children indoors and were to have their first meal inside the cabin. A somewhat chagrined Sarah quickly realized that cooking on the wood cookstove would take practice but no one seemed to mind that their peach fritters were slightly burned.

The afternoon saw the boys on the roof repairing some damage to the shake shingles. Grandpa had discovered on the previous day a stack of replacement shingles in the work room in the barn. There was not a moment of that day that passed by that Grandpa did not appreciate his brother Charlie. He had always admired Charlie's talents, but now he was to be direct benefactor of the work of his skilled hands.

Grandpa had not ceased to wonder about Charlie's whereabouts and his mind, turning over the various pieces of evidence they had, played an endless tune, "Charlie, Charlie, where are you....?"

He could have also played the same tune about the children's father. He prayed for them both throughout each day and tried to make some sense out of the two missing men. Just what was God trying to teach them in all of this?

As the afternoon wore on, Grandpa noticed a decided chill in the air and soon a shadow was falling over the yard as heavy clouds moved across the mountain.

Calling to the boys to try to get finished if they could, Grandpa loped off to bring in a supply of wood. As he rounded the woodshed, he noticed a distinctive spot of green. He grinned broadly. He knew the shape of those leaves very well. Before this night was over, he and the others would be feasting on creasy greens.

Upon depositing his armload of wood on the back porch, Grandpa called to Jessie, who was enlisted to harvest the greens. Before she had finished, the wind had really begun to blow and Grandpa called the boys off the roof and the three began laying in a goodly supply of Charlie's logs.

The mattresses, which had been airing on the porch, were brought in and the beds made. The boys were then sent back to the cave for the remaining blankets and possessions. Grandpa glanced at the sky with some concern. If he didn't know better....

Soon, the boys had returned laden with their final belongings. The temperature had really dropped by now and Grandpa added more wood to the fire—also lighting a fire in the fireplace at the end of the room.

Both girls were glad of this as they loved fireplaces, but Katy had begun to complain that she was cold. Then Josh squealed out with delight, "It's snowing!"

There was a mad dash to the window and excitement ran high, once again, as the swirling flakes descended to earth. "Grandpa, it's spring back home. Is this normal in the mountains to have spring-like weather one day and snow the next, especially this late in March?" Jessie asked with a little trepidation.

"Jess, the weather in the mountains is unpredictable. When I was growing up in Hazelwood, which is just two counties over, I have seen the worst snowstorms of the season as late as the end of April. This could just be a one-day occurrence or it could last for days and be blizzard conditions. Having no access to a radio, I just could not tell you what the forecasters are calling for," Grandpa hedged, trying not to show his concern, or reveal his gut feeling.

Suddenly, Sarah started signing wildly. She had discovered a radio while cleaning under Uncle Charlie's bed. Quickly running to retrieve her find, she returned with a triumphant look on her face.

"Charlie seemed to have thought of everything, now didn't he?" Grandpa asked of no one in particular.

Upon opening the battery compartment, however, his face fell. "Well, I thought it would be too good to be true if the batteries had held up. Instead they have leaked all over the connections. This will require some cleaning up before we can ever use it, if then," he stated flatly.

Upon seeing the downcast look on Sarah's face, however, he stated more brightly, "Jessie can pick up some batteries the next time she goes off the mountain and this will come in right handy in the future."

Soon, the evening meal was ready and Grandpa suggested a sentence prayer for their blessing. Around the table, the prayer went with everyone thanking God for His provision. Katy even thanked Him for a place to bathe her doll. The twins thanked Him for the 'tabin and Sarah, with shining eyes, signed her thanks that they were fulfilling their mother's request.

The meal was delicious! The creasy greens, in spite of their strong odor were a huge hit. Even the twins liked them. Grandpa attested that meals prepared over a wood cookstove were always better as they had to simmer longer and the flavors had time to bloom. If this was any indication of what he meant, then the whole family heartily agreed.

Whatever the reason, it was good and everyone attacked the fare with lusty appetites. Jessie noted with relief, once more, that Sarah's appetite and health had definitely improved since their trek up the mountain.

Talk around the table mostly concerned the snow and their new home, Uncle Charlie's cabin. Everyone seemed happy and content, and except for the pain of missing their mother and the yearning to see their father, Jessie was well pleased with their situation. She had worked hard to fulfill her mother's request and now that they were getting snowed in, she felt that she could finally relax. There would be time later to work at keeping food on the table, but tonight there was nothing she could do about that, so she gave in to ease and excitement over the falling flakes.

Everyone helped with clean-up, and soon they were relaxing close to the fire. "What a homey scene," Jessie thought as she looked around happily. Grandpa, who was sitting on a straight chair, had propped up a fat, sturdy log and stretched out his long legs until his stockinged feet rested upon it and were warming nicely in front of the hot embers.

Sarah, who was sitting in the rocking chair, was gently rocking the baby to sleep and Micah was stretched out on a quilt, mesmerized by the flames as they licked at the new pile of logs. Josh, the twins, Katy, and her doll were all lined up on the couch, grinning at one another as if they had a huge secret.

Jessie was seated on one side of the quilt, with her arms wrapped around her knees. Her mind was at rest finally and the warmth of the fire was melting the remaining tension in her muscles. It suddenly occurred to her that her persistent headache was gone. It must have been tension after all, she thought lazily. Well, maybe, it was gone for good as she relaxed here on this mountain.

Outside the falling flakes grew heavier and the wind had picked up considerably. The gusts rattled the windows and howled at the door. Inside, however, the family was safe and warm and grateful. Grandpa could only imagine what it would have been like to have stayed in the cave through this, with only brush to burn. As it was, they were safe and secure in a warm cabin with plenty of logs, and he could not stop breathing his thanks to his Maker.

Everyone periodically checked on the falling flakes and the snow was steadily piling up. Several inches had already accumulated, and great plans were being made to build snowmen and snow forts the next day. The twins chattered excitedly of their plans until the wind picked up and could be heard howling mournfully around the windows and doors. Then, their eyes open wide, they crawled to the quilt and sat in their big sister's lap. Jessie hugged them close and comforted them until an especially strong blast rattled the door, then she looked with large eyes at Grandpa. He just grinned broadly and said,

"Well, sounds as if that 'ole wind is trying to come on in here and warm itself by the fire, too. I always did like the wind. It can be soft and gentle and make you relax right into the most peaceful sleep you've ever known or it can be strong and gusty and push you around and make you feel like its going to lift you right off the ground. Right now its being pushy, but before you know it this same wind will be gently blowing your hair in a spring breeze, caressing your skin and making you feel good about yourself."

"Well, it's awful pushy, wite now," Tyler exclaimed in a most matter-of-fact tone.

"Yeah, pushy...." Ryler agreed as he turned his curly blond head and looked furtively over his shoulder at the door.

"Well, let's leave the wind to its pushy self and go take a much needed bath!" Jessie enthused.

Both twins jumped up and yelled, "Yeah!" as Jessie quickly ushered them from the room before they woke the baby. She just could not wait to get them in the bath tub and really clean again. She and Sarah had tried their best to keep them clean, but in their circumstances it had not been easy, so the fact that they had a bath tub again was a definite boon in her book.

Jessie scrubbed the twins until their skin shone pink and their blond hair, darkened from the water, hung in wet ringlets all over their heads. The twins, of course, wanted to play in the water, but Jessie reminded them that there were many others awaiting their turn for the bath tub.

Katy was next and, of course, her doll received a scrubbing as well. Jessie put the three little ones to bed and continued to dry Katy's long red hair vigorously with a towel, as Josh took his turn, to exit soon with that freshly scrubbed look, and clean wet hair.

Micah suggested that the girls go next as they were beginning to show the day's work by their tired looks. So, Sarah, then Jessie took their turns, and both girls could not remember when they had felt so good and clean before. They dried their long hair before the fireplace, then immediately went to bed to crawl between the sheets, which, though crisp and clean from hanging on the outside line, were cold, so the girls scooted close to Katy and snuggled together until all had drifted off.

It had been decided that the twins would sleep with Josh on the three-quarters bed tonight as the floor was so cold and so many blankets were needed. Grandpa planned to build the two little boys a small bed as soon as possible, but until then they all hoped that tonight's arrangement would work out all right. Micah, of course would take the cot.

Grandpa had kept the fire burning hotly in order to provide hot water for all the baths. He was so pleased with Charlie's ingenuity. He thought affectionately once again of his brother and how skilled he was in so many ways. One day they would learn of his whereabouts, he felt sure, and they would thank him for all the things that he had worked so hard to build all of these years, which were providing so well for all of these little ones right now. He just prayed that Charlie was all right, wherever he might be, and that this desire to thank him would, indeed, be possible someday.

What would Charlie think, Grandpa wondered, to see his house invaded as it was tonight with so many children, his great-nieces and nephews? Grandpa knew in his heart that somehow he would be pleased. In a roundabout way, it would be doing something for Amy, and Charlie never could refuse her anything.

Micah soon returned from his short stay in the tub and Grandpa headed in that direction himself. He planned to take a long soaking bath and soothe his sore muscles and aching joints. Being last definitely had its benefits.

Chapter Twelve

The boys were awakened the next morning to the twin's whispering. Then they remembered the snow and both boys scrambled from bed and crossed the cold floor boards to their respective clothes. They helped the twins to dress, and Josh complained cheerfully about all the kicking he had received during the night. All four were anxious to get down below where they were sure that it would be much warmer. The cold, however, had invigorated them and revved up their appetites. They could smell bacon frying and coffee boiling.

"Me 'opes we 'as tantakes!" Ryler enthused through his chattering baby teeth.

The boys descended the ladder to find Grandpa at the cookstove, turning the bacon strips. His hair was sticking out in several directions and he did not look that well rested. Micah decided then and there that he would bring the cot below before nightfall and Grandpa could sleep on it. He would take the couch and he and Grandpa could take turns keeping the fire going.

Grandpa cautioned the twins to be quiet as he wanted the girls to sleep as long as possible. They certainly needed their rest. The twins had trouble keeping their squeals down, however, as they peered out the window at the snow. It was higher than the level of the porch, which would make it close to a foot, and it was still coming down.

Micah immediately went out to bring in more firewood from the back porch. The wind was whipping the snow around and had piled it up in some pretty deep looking drifts. In spite of himself, Micah felt excited by it all. He was like a young colt. He wanted to run and kick up the snow, but the beginnings of manhood were forming in him and he determined to act responsibly. He felt good knowing that he was contributing to the family in a manner of responsibility, and he ensured they had plenty of wood before returning to the warmth of the house. He wanted his dad to be proud of him when he returned from wherever he was. A lump formed in his throat at the thought of his dad and he whispered softly into the wind, "Dad I am going to make you proud...."

As Micah returned to the living area, he heard the sizzle of the first pancakes as they hit the pan. He was again ravenous and could hardly wait to sink his teeth into them.

Josh was setting the table and finding a pan in which to make the sugar syrup. The twins still half-whispered excitedly at the window. It felt so good and homey that Micah's chest swelled within him. "If Mom...." Micah arrested that thought and washed up in order to help his grandpa finish the breakfast.

Soon the boys were seated around the table eating as many pancakes as Grandpa could fix. Their clatter and chatter eventually aroused the girls, who tumbled out of bed all sleepy-eyed to hug the fireplace.

Wonder of wonders, Annie had slept late, as well, and she was cooing and blowing bubbles contentedly now as she rested in Sarah's capable arms.

"I think sleeping in a drawer agrees with Annie," Micah stated as he moved in close to tickle her under her chin.

"I think you're right, Micah," Jessie rejoined. "Sleeping on that feather bed, however, is heavenly...." she said as she stretched luxuriously.

The girls and Grandpa settled down to their breakfast as Micah took over flipping the pancakes. Josh and the twins still chattered excitedly at the window, planning what they would do when the snow stopped.

When the others had their fill of pancakes, Micah dressed warmly once more and headed to the barn to check on the goats. The wind was blowing something fierce and the rock-faced mountain behind the barn was plastered with snow and icicles.

Micah's cheeks were becoming numb from the cold and the snowflakes were so driven that they stung his face, like tiny pinpricks, by the time he reached the barn.

Once inside, out of the wind, he felt better. The nanny goat shied away from his advances and the kids scampered about in fright, but once he carried an armload of hay to their stall, they ventured toward him hungrily. He knew, in time, he would win them over and he began mulling over what to call them. Then he decided that he would enlist the family to help name them. The little ones would enjoy that.

Micah closed the barn up tightly once again and headed back to the cabin by way of the woodshed. He would carry another armload of wood as he went. As he neared the wood pile, he was suddenly startled by a dark shape darting quickly away. The animal was shaped like a wolf and its dark fur was covered with snow. Micah watched as it disappeared suddenly into the white background, worry for the goat and her kids nibbling at him.

The girls were finishing the dishes as Micah swept the snow from his boots. His cheeks red from the cold, he moved to warm his hands by the open fire. The cabin was so warm and cozy. Micah realized that it already felt like home to him and marveled at the thought.

He looked at his sisters, who moved so gracefully, completing their chores in the kitchen. They looked happy. They looked like they belonged, too. He had never heard them complain about the work of helping their younger brothers and sisters. Micah's heart welled with love as he thought of their giving spirits. They all just pitched in and pulled together. They were a close family and he hoped that they always would be. They had lost their mother, did not know the location of their dad at present, but they were still a family and Micah meant to do his part in caring for them all.

When Micah could get a moment alone with his grandfather, he told him of the wolf-like animal at the woodshed. Grandpa's head came up and he looked concerned, then he said rather absently, "I wonder...."

The rest of the morning was spent watching the snowfall, preparing for lunch, and playing with the children. Jessie almost felt like they were on some kind of a vacation. Except for the obvious pain of missing their mother and father, they were happy and content. The fact that Jessie could relax now and not be concerned about the family being separated or discovered by Sean almost gave her a giddy feeling. That burden had been a very heavy one, indeed, for shoulders as young as hers, but she had relied on God and He had answered her prayers in a most surprising way. Jessie could hardly contain her praise to God and went about the cabin humming or sometimes singing her favorite hymns. Occasionally another family member would join in the singing and Jessie knew they were all feeling that wonderful relief and contentment of just being together.

After lunch, Jessie decided that they could get down to some serious business and broke out a jigsaw puzzle that she had found on one of her Uncle Charlie's bookshelves. With heads bumping, they pored over the pieces and soon the outside pieces had been found and assembled.

Jessie, seeing her grandpa nodding, suggested that he try out the feather bed. He agreed, with some prodding, and was soon sound asleep. Micah took that opportunity to climb the ladder and hand the cot down to Jessie and Josh. Tonight, Grandpa would rest better and the siblings smiled with satisfaction at the thought.

The family continued working on the puzzle, enjoying the warmth of their togetherness. They talked quietly or giggled softly as the twins tried repeatedly to fit pieces in where they did not belong. Jessie's heart felt full and complete as she worked contentedly on the puzzle with her younger brothers and sisters. She knew that her mother would be pleased and that somehow softened the pain of missing her.

Eventually, Sarah got up to start dinner and it was she who was the first to notice. She quickly approached the table again and rapped softly for attention. Then she signed excitedly that the snow had stopped. Chairs scraped backwards as a flurry of arms and legs tried to be first to the window. Sure enough, the snow had stopped.

"Tan we dough out now?" Ryler asked excitedly.

"I think that can be arranged," Jessie enthused. As the twin's volume rose, however, she quickly added, "If you will get ready to go out QUIETLY...."

"We will...." Tyler whispered in his most mature tone, his blond curls bobbing.

Soon, everyone was suiting up, including Sarah. Micah had dressed quickly and gone on out to measure the snow's depth. He opened the door and stuck his head in to announce, "Twenty-five inches of wet, sloppy snow!"

At that, Jessie added another pair of socks to the already encumbered twins. They looked ever so much like two roly-poly midgets, whose arms would not even comfortably go down to their sides. Jessie stood back to admire her work, however, and then ushered her wobbling little brothers on out the door.

Micah started shoveling a path to the barn and the twins began their play on the shoveled area as the snow was too deep for them to make their way around in it. Their mittened hands closed over wads of the wet, white stuff in an attempt to make snowballs. They only succeeded in throwing loose wads of the cold matter, however.

Josh began construction of the snow fort that he had envisioned. The snow was too sloppy, however, to stay together all that well. He finally resorted to just mounding it up.

Katy and Sarah had begun a small snowman and were having more success with their endeavors. Soon the twins began patting their "snowballs" onto the snowman and his foundation began to look lumpy, indeed. They all laughed at the structure and Katy began mounding and patting together "snow feet."

Jessie confessed that she had never thought of snow feet before, but soon their snowman had big ones sticking out from his ample foundation. Various items were retrieved for the features and sticks were brought for the arms. Jessie contributed the slouch hat that she had bought to wear to the village, and then before they knew it—they had a lumpy, bumpy snowman with feet!

By this time, Josh had built a pretty good snow wall and had crouched behind it with his store of sloppy snowballs, which he now began throwing in earnest. The twins and Katy started squealing and Jessie and Sarah began making their own to hurl back.

Grandpa had awakened by now and watched the foray with a hand on his chin and his body shaking with his chuckles. He turned from the window after a while and began preparing some hot chocolate. The kids would be in soon, chilled and ready to be warmed up from the inside out. He kept careful watch on the hot, foamy liquid, then moved it to the rear of the cook top and turned to stoke the fire.

Soon he heard much stamping and the door opened with a cold blast. His eyes locked with Jessie's as she inhaled deeply with appreciation in her eyes, and exclaimed, "Hmm, hot chocolate!"

Grandpa smiled and moved with gaited step to the cookstove to begin serving up the creamy liquid. The girls made short work of the wraps and began hanging the wet items near the fire to dry.

Soon the room was filled with not only the aroma of the hot chocolate, but also the smell of wet wool drying. Everyone was rosy-cheeked and warming their fingers around their hot cups. The steam, rising to their nostrils as they drank their brew, helped to thaw their noses. Everyone was happy and energized from their excursion into the white matter, and chattering excitedly.

The twins, of course, had to tell about the snowman they had helped to build and the snow balls that they had flung at Josh. Grandpa's eyes twinkled as he listened to their stories and remembered two other young boys who had played in the snow many times over throughout the years. Suddenly, he missed Charlie as he had not done in years and the lump that formed in his throat was truly a difficult one to swallow.

Chapter Thirteen

The next day saw the snow rapidly melting. The sun shone down warmly upon the white world and the wind blew briskly to the steady cadence of the melting snow dripping from the roof. The icicles, which had formed quickly the day before, were now falling with soft thuds.

Soon icy sheets were falling with a crash from the steeply pitched roof. At this rate, Jessie thought, the snow would all be gone by the morrow. Secretly, she was glad. She wanted to get back off the mountain and lay in some more supplies. She had made many plans the evening before as she sat up late talking with Grandpa and Micah.

Grandpa was to fix the hen house on the morrow, providing the snow kept melting at its present rate. Jessie and Micah were to go back off the mountain in search of chickens, piglets and possibly a small burro. Jessie was quite excited at the prospect.

The little ones wanted to go back out in the snow to play, but Jessie and Sarah both were firm about their decision that all would stay inside this day. There was too much risk of the snow from the roof, or the icicles that were still to fall, hitting the little ones and, the snow was a wet, sloppy mess today.

The older ones were hard pressed to curb the little ones' disappointment. Grandpa finally came up with the idea of drawing a garden diagram which would include a small patch for the youngest members of the family. Soon, the twins and Katy were busy planning their new garden, and Jessie and Sarah exchanged relieved looks with their grandpa.

Jessie was still praising her Lord for His provision for her family. She strongly suspected that her mother had known that last day that they would all be provided for by the God that she had trusted for so long. It was probably her prayers that had brought such a quick end to their real dilemma. Jessie's eyes teared up once again, as she thought of how very much their mother had loved them all. Even in facing her own death, she was thinking of them and trusting God for their future.

Micah soon returned from his trip to the barn with another steaming bucket of milk and their noon meal was served. Sarah was still trying to learn the intricacies of cooking on the wood cookstove, but she was making progress. Today, their navy beans and cornbread were cooked to perfection, however, and Sarah smiled her pleasure at their compliments.

After everyone had been served and had eaten their fill, Grandpa headed for the barn. He had plans to begin a cradle for the baby and he whistled as he trudged the mottled path to the tool room. It would not be the craftsmanship of Charlie's furniture-making, but it would serve the purpose, of that he was sure.

The older girls, after cleaning up from their meal, were sitting at the table once again, with blond heads bent, poring over their list for the trip to the village tomorrow. As Sarah signed, it was not as if they could merely turn around and go back if they forgot something, so they were using great care to think of everything. Also, they both knew that their money would soon be gone if they did not plan their purchases with care.

Josh was entertaining the little ones in the corner while the baby slept, so Micah ventured on out to the barn to see if he could help his grandpa. As Micah rounded the corner of the wood shed, he glanced up to the top of the rock face behind the clearing to see a dark shape bounding away. That creature, whatever it was, had chosen to remain around their clearing. Micah felt an unease where the little ones were concerned, whether they be animal or his own siblings. He thought of Uncle Charlie's gun which hung on a rack over the fireplace and prayed that he would not need it.

Micah and Grandpa had chosen to keep the information about the dark animal to themselves. They did not want to destroy the peaceful and contented feelings that they knew Jessie and Sarah were both feeling right now. The time, if need be, would come soon enough, but for the time being they opted not to worry the girls unnecessarily.

The afternoon passed quickly and the sun shone even warmer over the still white world. Patches of green had appeared and were growing larger by the time that sunset fell. The colorful sunset world, however, was made even more spectacular by the last rays shining off of the white patches and through the last lingering clouds.

Everyone had gathered at the windows when Micah had stomped in to report on the spectacular sunset that had temporarily reddened their world. The twins oohed and ahhed while the older members of the family tried to drink in the event. Jessie wondered if they would ever take for granted God's evening displays as the years marched by. She hoped fervently that they would always take time to appreciate their Father's handiwork.

That night after their evening meal and chores were finished, Micah strolled over to where Uncle Charlie's fiddle hung on the wall. "Grandpa, do you think Uncle Charlie would mind if I tried my hand at his fiddle?" Micah's eyes were fixed upon his grandpa's face to determine his true reaction to the question.

"Well, son, if you use proper care I don't believe he would mind a bit."

Hearing his grandpa's approval, a huge grin split Micah's face and he reached a young hand almost reverently to the neck of the antique fiddle. He slowly took it down from its hanger and reached for the bow. Then with great care Micah began to tune the instrument.

The little ones were quite interested in the process, but Grandpa's instructions to not touch were adhered to, albeit with much squirming to release the energy that the occasion generated.

After a while of tuning the instrument, Micah began with a tentative draw of the bow. The ensuing screech made the twins giggle and Katy, with green eyes shining, cover her ears.

Grandpa's memory of his brother's playing served him well and before the night was done, Micah had picked out one line of "Cripple Creek" on the old strings, with Grandpa's help.

"You seem to have inherited your uncle's flare for music, boy. I don't believe it will be too long before you will be serenading us," Grandpa observed with pleasure.

Micah was exhilarated by the experience and would have continued until the wee hours of the morning if Jessie had not called for bedtime. Micah went to sleep that night thinking of the trip to the general store on the morrow and the possibility of practicing the next evening, and while he did not realize it at that time, the pain in his heart had lessened ever so slightly.

Chapter Fourteen

The next morning saw Micah and Jessie stealing through the door of the tunnel with their empty packs on their backs, looking ever so much like two young teenage boys. Grandpa stood and watched them leave, whispering a prayer for their safety.

Coming out into the sunshine at the mouth of the cave, Jessie thought again how balmy the day felt already. There was still snow, of course, but the day was definitely a return to spring as the two youngsters set out to lay in their supplies.

The hike down the mountain was invigorating after being closed up in the cabin, and both siblings were up for the adventure of this day. There were still some icy patches in places, so extra caution was needed, but even with that it was only a little over two hours later that the pair came in sight of the general store.

Jessie pulled her cap a little further down over her eyes and made sure to slump her very straight back. She added a slight swagger to her walk and picked up a piece of straw to place in her mouth to chew. Micah would have laughed at these antics if it had not been done for the safety of them all.

The store owner looked up at the entrance of the two and Micah offered, "Howdy."

"Kin I he'p ya?" the owner asked while still surveying the two.

Jessie gulped really hard and thought, "It is now or never." Then she heard a voice she hardly recognized as her own telling the owner that they needed some supplies and would like to look around.

"Jest he'p yerselves and let me know when yer ready to chek out. Iffen ya need any he'p just holler—name's Otis, Otis Sneed," the owner called over his shoulder as he sauntered away.

Jessie inhaled deeply to calm her nerves and noted the strong smell of oiled wood. The old wooden floors creaked as she and Micah wandered around, checking out items. They pored over their list, almost agonizing over some of their choices in their zeal to stretch their money as far as possible. Finally, however, after much deliberation, the two settled upon their purchases, which consisted mostly of staples and made their way to the front of the store over the creaking boards.

Still eyeing the teenagers with blatant curiosity, the owner tallied up their purchases and Jessie paid the total. Then Jessie screwed up her courage to ask about the chickens.

Narrowing his eyes, the man slowly moved his meaty paw to his chin and stroking the same, turned slightly. Indicating the right hand side of the building, he told the two to check with his father-in-law next door. He just, "maught be able to he'p 'em."

Pressing her luck still further, Jessie turned as the two prepared to leave, laden down with their purchases. "What about ginseng, you know anybody in these parts who buys it?"

It was obvious from the owner's changed expression that she had struck a nerve.

"You'ns got sang for sale?" the man asked with interest.

"We might," Jessie nodded.

"Weil, now, I'd be iner'sted in seeing iny sang ye maught heve fer sale. You'ns jest bring it on by an' weil take a looksee." The owner watched them through narrowed eyes as the two made their way to the door.

"All right." Jessie, as she turned to nod once again, noticed the suspicious glint in the owner's eyes, but she continued with Micah to the white farmhouse next door.

Gaining the door, Jessie knocked for several minutes before a tall, thin woman, with stray wisps of hair playing about her face and wearing a plain work dress and apron, finally answered. She peered at the two furtively while she dried her work-worn hands on her kitchen towel.

"Sorry to bother you, ma'am," Jessie breathed, "we were just wanting to speak to someone about some chickens."

"You'd be wanting my father then," the woman offered. "He's around back at the barn. You boys just go on around there and holler fer him. His name is Caruthers, Pop Caruthers."

"Yes, ma'am. Thanks again for your help and we really didn't mean to bother you," Jessie apologized once more.

"Well, aren't you polite young men," the woman enthused, "and I ain't niver seen prettier eyes on a boy."

Jessie ducked her head at that and Micah scuffled his foot on the porch nervously.

"Well, best be going and thanks again," Jessie mumbled as she hurried off the porch.

On the way back to the barn, Micah gulped and chuckling softly stated. "Jessie, for a boy, you are acting a lot like a girl."

"Thanks a lot, Micah," Jessie shook her reddened face. "It's not easy to throw away a lifetime of being taught manners."

The necessity of calling for Mr. Caruthers was done away with as the two caught sight of the old man just exiting the barn with a goat in tow.

"Mr. Caruthers?" Jessie asked as the parties drew closer. "My name is Jessie and this is my brother, Micah."

"Whut's 'at? Zeke, did you say? And Michael? Weil I'm pleased to make yer acquaintance, young fellers," Pop Caruthers enthused warmly.

"Ah," Jessie began, but then stopped herself as she realized how she had so freely given their names and, blessedly, Mr. Caruthers mistake in understanding them.

"Mr. Caruthers...."

"You'ns can jist call me Pop. Ever'bidy else round here does."

"Well, thank you, Pop," Jessie began. "My brother and I were told that you might know where we could find some chickens."

"Weil, now, I maught at that. How many ye be wantin'?"

"Well, we thought to have two good laying hens...."

"Ye're goin' ta need a good rooster ta go with them hens."

"Yes sir, we will need a rooster, too. Do you know where we might be able....?"

"'Course, I got some hens an' a rooster if that's whut ye're wantin'."

"Well, we were looking for a good little burro, too, if you should know where we could get one." Jessie kicked at a clump of grass and spit for good measure.

"A burro, huh? Weil, I don't know 'bout no burro. How soon wuz ye needing one?"

"Today, if you...."

"Today! No I cain't he'p ya with no burro today! But, if you could wait a week or so, I maught be going trading an' we cud jist see."

"Well, I would be much obliged if you could help us find one...Pop...I certainly would." Jessie tried to squelch the hopeful look she felt creeping into her face.

"Weil, ya young fellers come back this time next week an' we'll see jist whut we kin do."

"That would be great, Pop," Jessie breathed. "We could just talk to you about the chickens then, too." Jessie certainly did not relish the thoughts of carrying chickens on their backs all the way up the mountain without the aid of the burro.

So saying, the goodbyes were dispensed and everyone looked forward to the next week when, hopefully, Pop would have been able to obtain a burro.

As they were walking away, Jessie suddenly remembered the piglets and turning back asked about those, as well, and Mr. Caruthers seemed to swell with this additional request.

Jessie and Micah began the long trek back up the mountain with the heavy packs upon their backs, little knowing the talk their presence had raised. The afternoon was thus spent by the owner and his family in conjecture about the presence of these two strange young men who apparently had such an interest in livestock.

Pop said they weren't up to no harm. Otis thought they bore watching and his wife defended them by saying they had good manners, no matter what anyone else said, and the oldest one surely had pretty eyes for a boy.

Chapter Fifteen

The following week saw the garden area laid off and life beginning to settle into a kind of pattern. The soil in the clearing at the base of the mountain was a rich, loamy texture though still mottled with stones, even with Uncle Charlie's obvious years of removing them.

Sarah had uncovered a book in Uncle Charlie's small bookcase which detailed certain mountain crafts, among which was the art of basketry. She was trying her hand at making a basket in the evenings to the progressing tune of Micah's "Cripple Creek."

Grandpa's pleasure at this homey scene each evening did much to help heal the deep wound of missing their mother. Jessie, wisely, wanted the healing to come, but at the same time did not want the little ones to forget their mother. This was a battle that raged within her during her few quiet moments. She resolved to hand these times over to the Lord and to concentrate upon HIS continuing goodness to them and for the most part she was successful.

The week passed quickly and before they knew it, it was time to make another trip to the general store. Micah and Jessie rose early again and began the hike for supplies, and, hopefully, this time, the livestock.

Stopping to rest at Shelter Rock, Micah remarked on what Jessie had already noticed. Spring was bursting out all over the place.

Wild flowers, which Jessie in no wise recognized, were blooming in profusion along the path. She stopped occasionally as she passed through some beautiful fragrance and tried to determine from whence it was emanating. Blue Flags she did recognize and delighted in the quantity and beauty of their blooms. She determined to dig some up on the way home to carry to Sarah and plant in their clearing.

Sooner than Jessie's nerves were ready, they found themselves entering the general store. Jessie breathed deeply of the now familiar odors and then fell to her task. Otis Sneed once again offered his services, but Jessie much preferred to look. She did not want to be talked into something which they could not afford, nor did she want Mr. Sneed to learn more about them than was necessary, so she deliberately chose to limit their contact.

Upon paying for their purchases, Jessie once again gathered her courage to ask, "Do you get much call for local crafts around here?"

"Weil, now, that depends. Whut kinda' crafts would ya' be meanin'?"

"Oh, baskets and carving and such...." Jessie ventured lamely.

"Baskets n' carvin', huh?" Otis eyed them steadily.

"You boys inta basket makin'?"

"Oh, no sir," Jessie stammered quickly. "We just know somebody who likes doing that sort of thing."

"Weil...ya' be bringin' me some o' them ther' baskets that SOMEBIDY likes doin' and weil see whut we kin do," Otis said as he rolled his wad to a different position and spit the brown liquid into a barrel he kept behind the counter just for the purpose.

Jessie thanked him kindly and then she and Micah turned to walk across to the farmhouse. A very red-faced Pop Caruthers strode onto the porch as the two siblings attained the screen door. Sweat ran down his face in rivulets and he removed his cap at sight of them and wiped his brow with his dirty sleeve.

"Is everything all right, Mr. Caruthers .... I mean 'Pop'?" Jessie asked with concern.

"Aa...Millie's done run off and I been chasin' her," Pop stated between breaths.

Jessie liked to have jumped out of her skin as Otis called out loudly just behind her, "That dern fool goat don't deserve to live!"

"Now, Otis," Pop stammered, "Millie's not sech a bad goat, she's jist adventooresome...."

"Adventooresome, my eye! She'd best not be in my storage shed agin, if'n she knows whut's good fer her!"

"Weil, I'm too tuckered to keer at th' moment!" Pop bellowed.

"I'll...." Otis began again only to be cut off by Jessie.

"'Pop, my brother and I would be glad to help you find Millie if your son-in-law doesn't mind watching our packs for us."

Otis' eyes flinched but he burst fort anew, "I don' mind watchin' yer packs, but if that blame goat has done iny more damag', we're having us som' goat stew 'is evenin'!"

Pop looked around and winked at the boys, and thanking them kindly for their help the three started out in pursuit of the errant Millie.

It didn't take long for the mischievous Nubian to be discovered but she had other ideas about going back into captivity. Micah showed his skills once again, however, and caught the bleating female but not without her showing some rage at her captor.

Pop soon had her calmed down, however, and the three headed to the barn with Millie submitting to her lead, and Pop expressing his thanks for their help.

"Millie don' went and got jellous when I brung that there burro home fer ya' boys, and took out her displeasure by runnin' off," Pop offered by way of explanation.

"So, you were able to get us a burro?" Jessie asked, forgetting to veil her joy.

"I said I's goin' tradin', now, din't I?" Pop asked almost incredulously.

Soon Millie had been contained and Pop, still huffing and puffing, brought out the burro. It was smaller than Jessie had envisioned but she soon thought that this might be better, as this way they would not need as much food for it.

Micah stepped forward and extended his hand to stroke the rough gray fur. The animal yielded docilely to his caresses. Then Micah attempted to open its lips and check its teeth as he had heard of horse traders doing. He heard Pop clear his throat rather loudly in the background in an attempt to swallow a chuckle.

Jessie knew absolutely nothing about burros other than that her grandpa had said that one was necessary. He had not felt comfortable with Jessie carrying all that weight up the mountain and he was determined to do something about it. Also, he had felt that a burro would be useful in other ways on their mountaintop.

While Jessie was lamenting her very ignorance of what to do, Micah suddenly had an idea and turning to Jessie he whispered, "I'll be right back."

While Micah loped off in the direction of the general store, Pop suddenly realized just how thirsty he was and he hollered rather loudly for his daughter Rachel to bring them something to drink. Besides, Pop was thinking of closing his deal and he liked to do these things hospitably.

Returning at a slower pace, Micah approached the burro once again lugging his heavy pack onto its back. With the exception of one ear flicking at a gnat, the burro hardly noticed his added burden.

"Do you think that he will accept the chickens as easily?" Jessie asked as she accepted, with a nod of thanks, a tall glass of ice water from the smiling Rachel.

"Weil, now, we kin soon find out, but first off we got t' git ya' set straight on yer sex." Pop rejoined as he downed the last of his water.

Jessie could have fallen over, her shock was so great, thinking that he meant HER, but before she could give herself away, Micah realizing her mistake and giving his "brother" a good-natured poke in the ribs saved the moment by addressing his attentions to the burro and saying they must call her Belle so that Zeke would remember in the future.

Pop, laughing with glee, said that he would go fetch the chickens so that they could gage her reaction, being female and all, you never could tell about them. So saying, he hobbled back through the barn to the chicken coops.

Micah, remembering himself, hollered after him asking if he needed any help. "A man kin a'ways use he'p," they heard Pop say in the distance and Micah handed his glass to Rachel with thanks and ran to catch up with her father.

"Zeke, is it?" Rachel asked pleasantly.

It took Jessie a full minute to realize that Rachel was addressing her and then she reddened significantly at the realization. She was still trying to recover from the close call that she had just had.

Rachel, however, if she noticed, only thought that the young man was embarrassed to be left alone with her. She continued brightly, "I wanted t' thank you boys fer helping Pop t' ketch that goat. Millie has been his special friend and project ever since Ma passed on. I would hate t' think o' somethin' happenin' t'her."

"Oh, don't think anything of it," Jessie replied, ducking her head. "We were glad to do it."

"You boys aren't from around here, are you?" Rachel queried and seeing Jessie duck her head again she hastened to add, "I mean you obviously are educated and all...."

Jessie colored again furiously and said in a soft voice, "We're from over in the next county." She was so thankful of their recent discovery, on one of Uncle Charlie's top shelves, of some survey maps which had indicated that the cabin was just across the line in the next county.

"Well, ya've come ta the right place to get yer livestock. Pop knows a great deal on that score. He spent all last week looking fer just th' right burro fer ya'. He said you'd be awanting a gentle un. Our piglets ain't weaned yet though, so'se you'll have to wait on that wish."

Still blushing considerably, Jessie expressed her thanks profusely and then thought how much like a girl it sounded. She could not meet this woman's eyes again because she was sure that she would see the truth. An uncomfortable silence ensued which was broken only by the arrival of Micah and Pop carrying between them a crate of two fat hens and a rooster.

"Now, they'll be off their layin' fer a day er two mos' likely, ya' know, with th' trauma of th' trip an' all," Pop was saying.

Micah and Pop strapped the crate of chickens on the back of the burro, who seemed totally unconcerned with the cacophony that she was to bear. "You'ns can be bringin' back my crate th' next time yer over ta this way."

"Oh, certainly, and we'll take good care of it, too." Jessie rushed to say.

"Tain't nothin' but a crate, son, don't reckin as how ya kin hurt it none," Pop said, eyeing Jessie curiously.

Jessie ducked her head again and said, "Well, I guess we'd better be settling up with you."

The trading then ensued and Jessie and Micah walked away with their burro and chickens feeling pretty good about things overall. The transaction had taken longer than they had expected, especially since they had helped catch Millie, but they were underway at last with their packs loaded on their backs and the feeling of a good deed done in their hearts. Jessie's face, however, did not lose its red glow until quite a bit later. Being a boy was going to be harder than she had realized and only last week she had thought what a nice touch it had been when she had added the spitting!

Chapter Sixteen

No one had considered just how to get the burro to the clearing. As a matter of fact, no one had even thought of it. That is because no one had ever lived in a totally inaccessible place. They were to find that would take some getting used to.

The best plan that Micah and Jessie were able to come up with, on the spur of the moment, was to tie the burro at the edge of the pasture where a spring head had greened the grass. Both had trepidation in leaving her there but did not know what else to do.

Maybe Grandpa would have a better plan.

The chickens were left in their coop temporarily in the cave until Micah could come back with Josh and Grandpa to get them. The duo hurried through the tunnel and arrived back at the cabin to find the youngsters all excited in hopes of seeing the new chickens and burro.

While Sarah and Jessie unpacked the backpacks, Grandpa, Micah, and Josh returned for the chickens and to do what they could to secure the burro for the night. Grandpa, too, was uneasy about leaving the burro untended but could come up with no better plan. He had wanted this purchase to take some of the burden off of Jessie, but, perhaps, they had been too hasty in their decision. At this point, all Grandpa knew to do was pray and that he did.

After a very tired Jessie and Micah had eaten their supper and related the events of the day, they took their respective baths and fell gratefully into their respective beds.

Micah found it difficult to fall asleep, he was so concerned about the burro, but Jessie not fully comprehending the dangers, slept like a log.

Up early the next morning, Micah went to fetch more wood for the fire and check on his chickens when to his unbelieving eyes, he saw the burro grazing peacefully on a clump of grass near the barn. Micah thought for sure he must be seeing things. He was even tempted to rub his eyes, but, no, it was Belle!

Forgetting all about the wood, Micah moved toward the burro speaking soothingly as he went. The goats, who were also grazing nearby, ran skittishly into the barn, but the burro only started slightly when they ran by her. Micah reached out his hand slowly to the burro on his approach, noting as he did the still dangling rope by which she had been tied. "How in the world...?" he thought.

Leading the burro on into the barn, he secured it in a stall and threw in some hay, then fetched a bucket of water. Afterwards, Micah stood in the yard surveying the perimeter. There was only a small almost imperceptible trail that the goats had used originally, which came down off the mountain, but how would the burro have known to use that? This was surely a puzzle.

Grandpa had come out onto the back porch for the forgotten wood by now, and Micah relayed the puzzling news to him. Grandpa stood scratching his head and wondering at this piece of news. Oh, well, he finally surmised, they had prayed but it was surely a mystery.

The kids all wanted to go see Belle as soon as they heard the news and she submitted to their caresses in her plodding, peaceful way. Grandpa would like to have met Pop Caruthers and thanked him for finding such a gentle animal for his family. He would just have to be content with feeling that way, however.

The rest of the morning found the family out in the clearing about their individual chores. Jessie was watching the little ones as she cleaned house. Micah, Josh, and Grandpa had plans to clear some more kudzu and lay off rows in the garden in preparation for planting potatoes the next week. The chickens were in their new hen house getting acclimated to their new surroundings. It was a peaceful scene.

Sarah wanted to be out in the sunshine today and with everyone's blessing had walked up onto the lower rocks to pick some spring flowers that she had noticed growing in the crevices. The yellow heads bobbed gently in the breeze as Sarah made her way slowly over the rocks. Micah, taking a break from his labor, noticed the graceful way his sister moved over the rough terrain. She definitely looked like a painting with her long work dress and her long ash-blond hair blowing in the breeze.

Micah returned to his labors and Sarah continued her climb, breathing in the warm spring air and enjoying herself as she had not done in a very long time. The views from every angle were beautiful beyond belief and Sarah reveled in the sheer beauty and wonder of their new home. Her only point of discontent was that she had not trusted God as Jessie had done. How He had provided! She breathed again deeply of the spring air and continued her slow, meandering climb.

Sarah was reveling, too in her new found strength. She had grown stronger in their short time at the cabin and her complexion, though still somewhat pale, was taking on a rosier hue. She was coming to feel up to the challenges of their new life. She was finding herself strangely suited to this existence. She wondered briefly if she had been born out of time, then chided herself that she should doubt God's timing. Trust was what she had been grasping for and trust was what she would ultimately do.

Wandering and wondering on her way, Sarah lost all track of time as she enjoyed this beautiful spring day. Jessie had insisted that she take some time to enjoy herself and that was just what she meant to do. Glancing back, Sarah saw Josh looking her way and waved to him in her delight, signing, "What a beautiful day!"

Josh signed back, "Ain't it, though!" and Sarah laughed her silent laugh of glee.

Suddenly, Sarah caught sight of some pink blooms just barely poking their heads around a big boulder in her path. She sighed with pure pleasure. One day she intended to know the name of every wildflower on the mountain, but today she had only to enjoy them whatever they were.

Sarah had come to the end of the boulders that she would be able to climb. To her right was the drop off the mountain, which was covered part of the way up with kudzu vines and straight ahead was more kudzu completely cutting off travel in that direction, and to her left was the rock face of the mountain. They were truly enclosed with rock and kudzu. Sarah determined, however, to go just a few more steps to more fully enjoy the pink flowers.

As Sarah moved cautiously to go around the boulder, she became aware of a buzzing. It sounded ever so much like a katydid and Sarah puzzled briefly about why a katydid would be out in the spring. Then she thought about the fact that Grandpa had said the old-timers believed that it would frost six weeks after the first katydid was heard. Why that would be sometime in late May, she thought, and laughed her silent laugh at the fact that this time the old-timers were wrong!

The buzzing grew incredibly loud suddenly and Sarah thought the noise was almost deafening. She had never heard a katydid be this loud before, although on a late summer night a multitude of them could sound deafening.

Micah, Grandpa, and Josh all had glanced up at the sudden loud buzzing. Micah looked at Grandpa with concern only to hear Grandpa yell, "Rattlesnake!" and glance in the direction of the noise to see Sarah's blond head jerk back with surprise.

"Get the gun!" Grandpa yelled as he loped off in Sarah's direction running faster than Micah would have thought possible.

Micah, himself, took off at such a run that he stumbled and fell twice only to keep moving through the falls. It seemed to Micah that it took forever to gain the house and note Jessie's startled face as he grabbed the gun from its rack and the box of bullets from their hiding place, quickly loading the gun.

Grandpa was gaining on Sarah as Micah, heart pounding, dug his toes into the soft earth lunging his way toward his sister. Suddenly, out of the corner of his eye, Micah saw a dark shape plunge down the face of the mountain, sliding on the sheer rock wall, headed straight toward Sarah.

Micah stopped mid-flight and raised the gun to his shoulder. Before he could fire, however, the wolf-like creature had leapt to the back side of the boulder that he had attained and Micah screamed to Sarah to, "Watch out!"

Putting himself into high gear once again, Micah gave it all he had to gain the boulders and his grandpa. He saw, as if in a dream, Sarah's hands fly up to her face in what he knew must be a silent scream. His mind suddenly exploded with, "God help us!"

Climbing hard, red-faced, and gasping for breath, Micah finally reached his grandpa, who had suddenly stopped in mid-stride. Raising the gun once again, Micah trained it on the wolf only to have Grandpa suddenly wrench it from his grasp. He heard a yelp of pain and Grandpa yelled, "Sarah, stay down!" And raising the gun and taking careful aim, he fired once.

Sarah was collapsed in a heap and Grandpa moved forward as rapidly as possible over the boulders. The wolf-like creature moved slowly toward Sarah and stood staring at her. Micah wondered distractedly why Grandpa did not shoot it but Grandpa was moving at an angle away from Sarah. Suddenly he raised the gun again and shot down at the rocks below him. Micah saw Sarah raise her hands to her ears and he moved immediately to her side. As he approached, the wolf eyed him with an intelligent look and suddenly turned and disappeared behind the boulders.

Sarah was crying hysterically by this time and Micah, not knowing what else to do, just hugged her and tried to calm her down. Josh suddenly let out a war whoop and exclaimed,

"Grandpa! That is one huge snake!"

Jessie was approaching the scene by now and Micah thought to ask Sarah if she had been struck. Shivering violently, Sarah shook her head vehemently and mouthed, "No!" Sarah was shaking so badly that she could not stand, so Micah moved aside and let Jessie through so that she could comfort her sister. Sarah cried afresh at sight of Jessie and the two clung together.

Grandpa had sent Josh back for a hoe by this time and he turned around to say with emphasis, "Be on the lookout. These things generally travel in pairs!"

Jessie and Micah immediately scanned the surrounding area. Sarah was too upset to do more than sit and cry. "Grandpa, why didn't you shoot the wolf?" Micah asked with incredulity.

"Because, son, that wolf saved your sister's life...." Grandpa returned in a thick voice.

Micah whirled around and faced Sarah. "Is this true, Sarah?"

Sarah affirmed by nodding vigorously. Then she tried to sign the details but she was shaking too hard for control. As Jessie stood and realized Grandpa's intention with the hoe, which Josh was running to fetch, she stated in a firm voice, "Sarah, Micah and I are going to take you back to the cabin."

With the help of her brother and sister, Sarah was finally able to stand, but they had almost to support her between them, where they could to get her back to the cabin.

She was horribly upset by her experience and Jessie did not wonder at that. She perfectly understood. A rattlesnake and what Sarah believed to be a wolf, both coming at her at the same time! That was just too much for any girl to handle!

Finally, Sarah's shaking had diminished somewhat and by the time that Grandpa and Josh appeared on the scene, she was able to relay her side of the story.

She had been reaching down to pick one of the pink flowers when she had heard the buzzing. Not until the buzzing had become almost deafening, however, did she realize that something was wrong. Then she had seen the snake with its thick body in coils prepared to strike. She had been frozen with fear when suddenly she had been aware of something moving rapidly toward her and had just caught sight of what she believed to be a wolf when the rattler had struck at her. Reflexively she had fallen backwards. The wolf had caught the rattler in mid strike, however. The rattler had struck with a flat mouth (Grandpa had interrupted at this point to state that the rattler had unhinged its jaw) and Sarah had seen the fangs which had only been about four inches from penetrating her leg when the wolf had caught the rattler. The snake was so long that the wolf had about three feet of snake at the head end. The snake had whirled around and struck the wolf in the head, but Sarah did not think that the fangs had gone in as it was a glancing blow and she had seen the venom running off of the animal's muzzle.

The wolf had barely flinched when Grandpa had fired the gun at the rattler but had simply stood and stared at Sarah, almost as if to ascertain that she was all right. It had continued to stare at her until Micah had gained her side, then it had turned and disappeared as rapidly as it had appeared.

Micah's and Grandpa's side of the story had to be told as well, and it was soon past lunch time, but no one noticed. Grandpa then rose to do what he called "a messy chore" and Micah left to go with him as he headed out the back way. Sarah continued to sit on the couch and tried valiantly to calm herself completely down. Jessie served up lunch to the little ones and glanced over in the midst to find Sarah in a deep slumber. "Good," she thought. "I hope she sleeps all afternoon. She has earned it."

Jessie maneuvered the little ones outside after their meal so that Sarah could have a quiet cabin in which to sleep. The group, however, stumbled upon Grandpa and Micah and their "messy chore" as they wandered around back.

Grandpa had skinned the snake and now he and Micah were finishing up the stretching process on the side of the barn where they intended to dry the skin. Grandpa, by way of explanation, said that a six-foot skin should fetch a pretty fair price of any man's money. Jessie at that point wondered just what all they would eventually be selling in order to provide for their family. Her qualms lessened, however, in light of the trade-off of provisions.

Later in the afternoon, Grandpa and Micah built a little fire in the fire pit outside and skewered the snake meat. The aroma of the meat roasting over the hot coals was soon overpowering. Micah, Josh and Grandpa partook of the fare, but the girls said, "No, thank you," in no uncertain terms.

After the others had gone in, Micah was watching the last rays of daylight as he made sure that the fire was out. He heard a slight rustle behind him and turned just in time to see a dark head poking around the side of the shed. He half stood and then he grabbed a hunk of the left-over rattlesnake meat and tossed it toward the shed saying softly as he did, "Eat it, Wolf, you have earned it...." and with that he called it a day. Leaving the rest of the meat behind, as well, he provided Wolf with a hero's meal.

Chapter Seventeen

Jessie was awakened near dawn the next morning to soft moaning. After a few moments of orienting herself, she realized that it was Sarah, obviously having a bad dream. She reached over the sleeping Katy and shook Sarah gently. When this did not awaken her, Jessie reached for the flashlight which was lying on the floor beside the bed and using its beam to locate the matches, lit the oil lamp. As its soft glow lightened the dark room, Jessie saw Sarah, still deeply asleep and moaning. Her face was bathed with moisture.

Jessie crept around to Sarah's side of the bed and once again tried to rouse her sleeping sister. This time she was successful and Sarah awakened with a start, her eyes wild with fright. Jessie smoothed the damp locks back from Sarah's face and Sarah, perceiving Jessie's own face in the lamplight, sighed with relief as tears began their descent down her face.

"It was just a nightmare, Sarah...." Jessie soothed.

Sarah raised her trembling fingers to sign, "It was a horrible nightmare!"

"Do you want to tell me about it?" Jessie asked quietly.

"Oh, Jessie," Sarah signed weeping, "I dreamed about that rattler."

"Sarah, Grandpa killed that rattler. You don't ever have to worry about it again," Jessie stated emphatically.

"But, Jessie," Sarah signed fearfully, "I dreamed that rattler was only one of many."

At that, Sarah broke down in sobs and Jessie quickly knelt and wrapped her arms around her trembling sister only to find herself being pushed away as Sarah sought to sign her agitation. "Jessie, you do not understand...just as that rattler struck at me in my dream, Mama reached out and...." Sarah was sobbing so hard that she was not able to finish.

"You dreamed about Mama, too?" Jessie asked with compassion as the tears started streaming down her face now, as well.

Sarah nodded her head pitifully. Then she began her signing again, between hiccupping sobs, "I dreamed...that Mama reached out...and grabbed the rattler just as it reached me...."

"Oh, Sarah...."

"Jessie .... the rattler turned into Uncle Sean!" Sarah signed vehemently, her eyes wide with fright.

"Sarah, it was just a dream. A horrible dream...." Jessie soothed.

"There were other rattlers in the background. They were all coiled and ready to strike Mama and I could not scream a warning. I was too scared to move so I could not sign, and she could not see me if I had signed." Sarah, signing rapidly, was really distraught now.

"You have to calm down, Sarah. You are going to make yourself sick. No rattler can hurt Mama now, so you don't have to worry about that. And Sean will never find us here. He never paid any attention to family doings, so he doesn't even know the area where Uncle Charlie lived." Jessie was trying desperately to calm her sister, but suddenly she thought, perhaps, this was just what Sarah needed, to cry it all out.

Jessie once again wrapped her sister up in her arms and Sarah cried until she could cry no more. The rays of morning came softly stealing in the window, finding the two sisters crying out their sorrow one more time.

Finally, Jessie felt Sarah's grasp slackening and she gently disengaged her arms and lowered the nodding Sarah onto the feather bed. Then, going to the washstand, she splashed some cold water onto her face and readied herself to face another day.

Sarah's sobbing had done something to Jessie. She had finally released that last bit of deep grief that she had been holding back. She knew that she would still miss her mother and probably cry for her from time to time, but the deep grief was finally cried out.

She prayed that the same might have happened to Sarah, as well.

Jessie felt strangely unburdened and ready to face the challenges of the future. She knew at last that she had accepted God's answer concerning her mother. He had a different plan for their lives now, but He had certainly used their mother to help shape all of their lives, and her presence would always be felt in a big way because, in essence, she was a very real part of them. That was a comforting thought.

Feeling in her heart that Sarah was going to be fine now, Jessie thought of the dream and all the factors interwoven in it. She had no doubt but that Sean was following the leading of the Old Serpent and that her mother's prayers had averted disaster there. God had sent the wolf to further avert disaster when he caught the rattler in his own jaws. Jessie just felt such a peace in her heart that God would always be there for them in one way or another. What a GOOD God they served! Jessie went about her early morning chores with pure praise in her heart once again.

Grandpa noticed Jessie's swollen eyes and radiant look and only asked if she had slept well. "Sarah had a nightmare about the rattler," Jessie gave her reply to Grandpa's questioning look.

Nodding slowly, Grandpa looked into the distance before replying, "Sarah always seems to bear the brunt of things, don't she?"

"That's true, but talk about a phenomenal rescue!" Jessie shook her head again with the wonder of it all.

The others, with the exception of Sarah, were soon up and another day on the mountain began in earnest. Everyone now had their assigned chores and fell to their responsibilities. Micah headed to the barn to stake the burro out to graze and allow the goats their freedom. Josh and the twins had taken to feeding the chickens and checking for eggs. Grandpa had determined to let one of the hens set and so at present they were only getting one egg a day but that was keeping them in pancakes, so no one complained.

Grandpa had finished the twins' new bed and was working on the cradle for the baby in addition to all of his other chores, which included helping Micah carry wood to the back porch and working on the garden.

Jessie had planned a half day off today, however, in light of yesterday's excitement. She planned to pack a picnic lunch and take her family to the flat rock in the field where they had first dined on the mountain. Today marked one month that they had been in their new home and she meant for them all to celebrate.

Toward noon, Sarah finally awakened and the two girls packed their lunch, and gathering their family began the trek to their picnic spot. It was a lovely spring day and everyone was ready for the fun they planned to have. Micah went first and scouted out the area to make sure that no one was about. The younger ones had been cautioned to be quiet, but other than that everyone meant to relax and enjoy themselves. Jessie knew that this was not something that they could hope to do often, but today being so special, she thought it would be all right.

The twins ran through the meadow like wild Indians, Josh in hot pursuit. Katy had elected to help set up the picnic and finding the perfect spot for her rag doll, Bessie, she wanted to help like the big girls. Grandpa leaned back against the little tree and Micah, after offering his help, just stood and surveyed the happy scene.

The picnic was soon served and the family lounged for some time, talking about the events of that first day on the mountain and the ones that had led up until today. They could see God's leading through it all, and it helped to see the events in perspective.

Jessie was lying on a quilt in the grasses, with the sleeping Annie at her side, letting the sun lull her into an afternoon nap.

Grandpa had been snoring rhythmically for a little while and Micah had joined Josh in another merry frolic through the meadow with the little ones. Sarah had walked a short distance from the sleeping party to try to overcome her fear of seeing another snake. She meant to bone up and be able to face any future challenges with more maturity and grace. She was determined.

Sarah turned back to survey the face of Castleknob. She found it to be creating in her a sense of security, knowing what she knew—that it had invited them in and secluded them. No one could possibly detect the truth by looking at this formidable facade. That a cabin was nestled safe and secure on the back side of this mountain was something that simply could not be guessed.

Shading her eyes to gain a better view of each crevice and outcropping, Sarah tried to memorize what she saw. Maybe she would try her hand at painting it, so she paid particular attention to all of the elements that went into giving this mountain its castle look.

As she continued to gaze and take in the incredulity of the sight, her eyes suddenly focused on a small movement. A dark shape was weaving its way in and out of the boulders. Sarah squinted in her efforts to make out the shape. She continued staring until she knew. She well knew that shape and she gulped hard and started to bolt when she remembered her resolve—and planting her feet firmly, she waited for the event to unfold.

Then Sarah smiled a special smile. The mystery was solved. The dark wolf-like shape continued toward her now only stopping now and then to give the rope another tug to make sure that Belle still followed. So that was how Belle had reached the clearing that day! Sarah suddenly knew that this was no wolf that was leading their burro in a way that they knew not.

Feeling only minor trepidation, Sarah stood stock-still as she recognized, what must surely be a very intelligent dog, leading their little burro straight to her. When the dog, which still looked so much like a wolf, was three feet from where she stood, it stopped and looked earnestly into her eyes. Sarah reached out a slightly trembling hand and the dog approached slowly until it had placed the rope into her grasp. Then Sarah did, what was for her a very brave thing. She reached with her other hand to stroke the animal's dark fur. The creature submitted freely to her caresses, then sat and lifted its paw. Sarah reached under its muzzle to gently grasp the proffered handshake, thinking as she did so that this animal must surely have belonged to Uncle Charlie.

The rest of the family members were greatly surprised a little later to look up and see Sarah leading their little burro toward them, followed at a short distance by the wolf-like creature. She signed quickly that it was friendly and had led Belle straight to her. The incredulity of the family was great, but the proof was in the pudding.

Then Sarah handed Belle's rope over to Micah and turning, she knelt and indicated to the wolf-like dog to come to her. Eyeing the others furtively, he slowly made his approach. Upon gaining Sarah, he sat obediently and looked into her eyes turning his head quizzically. The rest of the family looked on dumbfounded.

Then Ryler piped up, "Tan I pet 'ou dog, Saywa?"

Grandpa intervened quickly, "Ryler, let's let Sarah's dog get a little more used to everybody before we shower him with caresses."

Micah thought of the leftovers from the picnic then and, handing the rope to Josh, he retrieved the scraps and slowly made his way to Sarah and the dog. "Would you like some more food, Wolf?" he asked softly.

Wolf sniffed the air but did not leave his position in front of Sarah. Micah soon knelt beside Sarah and set the scraps on the ground in front of the dog. Taking a look at Sarah, as if to ask permission, Wolf downed the scraps with decorum.

Sarah then turned to Micah and signed that Wolf did seem the appropriate name and so Wolf he became.

Soon the picnickers, leaving no trace that they had been in the meadow, began their trek back home. Belle was left tied to the little tree in hopes that Wolf would, once again, do the honors of leading her home and sure enough, a short time later she appeared back in the clearing. Now Jessie and Micah could head down the mountain tomorrow in hopes of finding seed potatoes amongst the other needed supplies since Belle could now be depended on to lug the heavy bag of potatoes back up the mountain.

That night an old pan was found and cleaned and filled with scraps for Wolf. The next morning, he was discovered sleeping on the back porch next to the woodpile and the bonding with this intelligent creature began in earnest.

Chapter Eighteen

The family worked hard in the coming weeks planting their garden and continuing the clearing of the kudzu, with their general upkeep and individual chores, as well. In the midst of all of the work, Micah kept to his practicing of Uncle Charlie's fiddle, and Sarah continued to make baskets, however.

Sarah's first attempts at weaving the kudzu vines into baskets had left a lot to be desired, but she was finally getting the knack of it and was close to turning out some work which she and Jessie felt they might be able to sell.

Grandpa's carving was coming along, too. He had not carved in years, but he was proving to have been a craftsman at one time and his skill was returning. Jessie had watched these enterprises with alacrity as she knew that their money would not last much longer and something had to be done to create income.

Micah was becoming more adept at bringing home rabbits and squirrels for stews. He was careful with the skins, too, as he was trying to think of some way to use them for profit in the future.

They were getting some early produce from their garden in the form of spring onions, radishes, and small leaves of lettuce now. The creasy greens had provided them with side dishes for a while as they had been careful to harvest the leaves before they became too bitter, which had resulted in more growth. Also, the volunteer potatoes were yielding a crop of small potatoes now, both red and white.

Grandpa had wandered into the woods one day and come back with a small harvest of fiddleheads, which none had ever eaten but most enjoyed. Micah had tried his hand at fishing a number of times by now, and on a few occasions they had enjoyed trout stew.

The eggs under the setting hen were due to hatch out any day now, and the little ones were excited about the fuzzy baby chicks to come. Jessie was more excited about the prospect of more eggs.

Some days she dreamed of having a fried egg for breakfast. Blessedly, the little ones had not tired of pancakes and oatmeal, but she was keeping her mouth set for fried eggs with bacon one day soon.

Grandpa had discovered that if he hacked down aways, he had been able to find ham that was still good of those hanging in the smokehouse. That had been a big boon to their meals and had provided seasoning for their constant fare of dried beans. All in all, they were still eating pretty well.

The nanny goat had weaned her kids now and so their milk supply had increased quite a bit. Jessie had been very relieved about this as now they could feed the baby on goat milk exclusively. They had mixed it with formula for a while until the formula had run out. Jessie in no wise wanted to be buying formula from the Stekoah General Store. She did not want anyone to know about the baby. That would be too much of a clue. She and Micah had bought plenty of formula at the grocer's the day of the sale of Jessie's car, so no formula had ever been purchased at Stekoah.

God had provided so well for them, and the family, at their blessing time each evening, thanked Him faithfully for His goodness to them. Jessie well knew that they could never have done this without God's care.

Wolf had continued to worm his way into the family's heart, but he was definitely Sarah's special friend. She could not go out of the house without Wolf's faithful companionship. The rest of the family breathed a collective sigh of relief at this as they well knew that if Sarah should ever need assistance, she, of course, would not be able to call for it. Now they could relax some, where Sarah was concerned.

Jessie walked out on the porch to rock the baby and feast her eyes upon the view. She hoped she would never grow tired of absorbing the beauty of this very special place. She could hear the rhythmic thuds and cracks of Grandpa splitting wood, the maaing of the baby goats, Josh and the twins' squeals as they played hide-and-seek, the clatter of the plates that Sarah was putting up in the kitchen, and Katy who was sitting in the other rocker on the porch, singing softly to her rag doll, Bessie. These were family sounds - wonderful music to Jessie's ears.

She thought about Micah and how he might find fresh meat for them for dinner. The baby cooed softly as she lay in Jessie's lap, gazing upon her sister with heavy lids. A bee flew into her range of vision and Annie's eyes flew open wide for a moment. Jessie laughed softly and thought of the bee gums at the edge of the property which Grandpa had cleaned, hoping for a fresh hive to move into them.

Honey would be a wonderful commodity to have, lessening their need for the purchase of sugar. Jessie thought, too, of the sugar peas that would be ready for harvest soon. She had plans to just sit in the row and open a few pods and eat the raw peas then and there. They had such a wonderful, nutty flavor when eaten raw.

Grandpa and the family had planted a number of rows of corn. They planned to dry the corn and take some of it to be ground into meal. Jessie's mouth watered, thinking of the cornbread that would come of that. Cornbread was one of her favorite things and she was glad as they ate so much of it. Of course, they did not have the luxury of butter right now, but maybe in time that would come, too.

Jessie was appreciating this time of ease. She knew only too well that once the garden started to come in, then she and Sarah would become very busy, indeed. But today, with the warm breezes blowing up from the valley, she would relax and just enjoy her baby sister until she fell asleep.

Glancing over at Katy, Jessie smiled with affection to note that Katy was the one who had fallen asleep and her doll was as wide-eyed as ever. Sarah came quietly to the door and looked out upon the scene, breathing deeply with satisfaction. Jessie knew that domestic responsibilities gave Sarah a deep sense of peace and joy. She did not seem to have the dread of housework that Jessie confessed to having. Jessie would rather be outside. Sarah seemed to thrive on caring for the house, though she did enjoy planting flowers, too. The blue flags that Jessie had brought her were now thriving not far from the back door.

Sarah came on out onto the porch, quietly closing the screen door behind her. She gracefully lowered herself onto the porch step and Wolf came to lie beside her. She gazed lazily upon the blue of the distant mountains and sky, then turned to sign to Jessie,

"I cannot believe how tranquil it is here...."

Jessie gave her agreement with a lazy nod of her head. Then she signed to Sarah in order not to awaken her sleeping sisters.

"We're going to have to think of schooling by this fall."

Sarah grimaced slightly then signed, "It will be good to be studying again, but let's think of summer vacation right now."

Jessie chuckled softly and agreed. Schooling would wait until later. After all, had they not been getting a very real education in life itself over the last months?

Chapter Nineteen

Annie had fallen asleep at last, so Jessie rose to put her back to bed and decided to treat herself to a walk. There was really no question where her feet would take her, but she only signed to Sarah as she left that she was going to take a walk.

Breathing deeply of the fresh spring air, Jessie stood on the opposite side of the waterfall, gazing upon the beauty of the scene below her. The lower section of their rock-faced mountain was dotted with a profusion of pink and white blooms of the mountain laurel and rhododendron. While these thickets made travel very difficult at times, they were incredibly beautiful when in full bloom as they were now.

Sarah had decorated their cabin for the past week with cuttings from these beautiful shrubs with their glossy leaves and their unusual blooms. There were, also, the yellow, orange, and deep tangerine blooms of what Grandpa had called the mountain azalea which dotted the mountain and now their new home with Sarah's arrangements, which included lacy ferns.

Jessie continued to gaze upon the incredible beauty before her as she lost herself in the roar of the waterfall beside her. Her tired muscles were relaxing as if caressed by this music and occasionally a breeze would blow the refreshing mist into her face, and she would close her eyes with delight.

How blessed they were!

Standing thus in her reverie, Jessie barely caught the sound of the footsteps moving up behind her. She smiled to herself and then said, "So you found me, Sarah?"

Sarah moved up and gracefully wrapped her sister in a hug and stood surveying the beauty below with her. When Jessie finally turned to face her, Sarah signed, "How did you know it was me?"

Shaking her head with amusement, Jessie said, "The same way I always know it is you, Sarah. By the soft clicking on the rocks of Wolf's nails that seems to accompany you wherever you go."

Laughing her silent laugh, Sarah reached down to give her constant companion a playful pat. Wolf looked up with those trusting eyes and both girl's hearts melted once again.

"So, how did you know where to find me?" asked Jessie.

Signing gleefully, Sarah indicated that was the easy part. She knew this to be Jessie's favorite spot—but also, Wolf had given her away by continuing to look in the direction of the waterfall. She had just naturally followed.

"What are we fixing for supper tonight?" Jessie asked as she knelt to shake Wolf's lifted paw.

"We are having cream of asparagus soup, with a few spinach leaves thrown in for good measure, corn dodgers, and strawberry pie....IF the kids pick enough wild strawberries today!" Sarah signed emphatically.

"Um...sounds wonderful...." Jessie was hungry already. That was the thing about living on a mountain. You seemed to stay hungry all the time no matter how much you ate! They had all developed healthy appetites since making their home here.

"You know, Sarah, isn't God wonderful?" Jessie asked as she gazed lazily into the distance. "He knew we were going to be living here before the beginning of time and he has been planning for our arrival all this while. He had Uncle Charlie plant more than he knew he would ever need, even though HE didn't know anything about our coming to live here. We will be eating from that asparagus bed for five to six weeks according to Grandpa, and then we should have strawberries for a while since Uncle Charlie cultivated both wild and tame berries. Grandpa said those are raspberry canes that have put out so well and what with the blueberries, huckleberries, and gooseberries— we can have pies all summer. In spite of losing most of the peach blooms to the cold, we may still have some peaches and the pear, apple, cherry, and plum trees were so beautiful when they bloomed, and if all goes well we should have a fine crop from each."

"Can you believe just how blessed we are? If only we had Mama and Daddy here it would be just perfect...but Mama would not want to come back to earth even if she could, and Daddy will join us here one day soon. In the meantime, how can we help but to be happy in a place like this that is supplying our needs in more ways than we could have imagined?" Jessie breathed all of this out with incredulity but true praise for her Lord in her heart.

Sarah just smiled her special smile and continued stroking Wolf's dark fur. She admired her sister greatly for her faith that had helped to sustain them all and now her unbridled gratitude. Sarah's long, ash-blond locks blew gently in the breeze as she reclined against the rock outcropping and soaked in the sun's rays. She had never believed that she could be happy again after her mother died, but here she was content with her life and happy in the knowledge that her mother was happier than she had ever been while she had been upon this earth, and she had been pretty happy here. It was a marvel to Sarah.

"Well, enough relaxing," Jessie said as she surveyed her beautiful spot once more. "We had better go and rescue those strawberries if we are going to have any for a pie tonight!"

Sarah laughingly arose and the two girls headed back to the cabin discussing their grocery list for the morrow's trek off the mountain.

The next day proved to be another beautiful spring day, which Jessie knew that she and Micah would be sure to enjoy considering the profusion of blooms that they would pass on their way down and then back up the mountain. The two headed out and Wolf, as he had done now for weeks, brought Belle to them shortly after they exited the cave on the other side.

The hike down seemed effortless now after so many trips and Jessie delighted in the strength of her legs. But today, they lingered some on the trail and admired all of the spring flowers which were a regular riot of colors.

Once Jessie squealed out with delight when she spied a bit of yellow through the branches of a tree, and upon turning aside to examine it, discovered a pristine patch of yellow Lady's Slippers. She stood admiring them for some time until duty called her away and she promised herself that she would bring Sarah back on the morrow to see them.

With so much to see, the time passed swiftly and they were at the general store before they knew it. Since the purchase of Belle, they had taken to entering the store separately as Micah would take the burro to the side of the building in order to tie her while they made their purchases. Today, they were bringing four of Sarah's baskets and two wood carvings of Grandpa's for Otis to inspect with the possibility of purchasing. As their money was almost at an end, it was very important that they begin selling the baskets and the carvings soon. Jessie had great confidence in their products, but she did not have as much confidence in her ability to sell them for a fair price, so she was a bit nervous on this day.

She went into the store and greeted Otis, then she began walking around on the creaking boards making her selections. She was crouched down on the floor looking at something on a bottom shelf on the second aisle when she heard the screen door slam. She moved to straighten so that she could let Micah know where she was when her heart leapt into her throat. She would know that voice anywhere, but she would never have believed that she would have heard it here. It was Sean! Sean making small talk with Otis. Jessie froze in place and then started as she realized the trap that Micah was just before walking into. She cast frantically about in her mind for a way to warn him. She lacked the courage to just run out past her uncle, but she had to warn Micah. She arose shakily and walked as casually as she was able to the window which faced out to where Belle was always tied.

Blessedly, Micah was still standing beside the burro, apparently having trouble with the rope that had bound the baskets to the faithful back. Jessie, with her back turned to the talking men, tried frantically to gain Micah's attention. Micah had finally untied the baskets and grabbing two in each hand was turning to head to the front door of the store. Jessie frantically motioned to him, but he did not see. Just as she despaired of ever gaining his attention that way, Belle hee-hawed which caused Micah to turn to see what was the matter and in so doing, he caught the movement at the window. Jessie could have cried with relief when Micah saw her. She quickly signed to him, "SEAN — HERE!"

Micah looked at her quizzically, then she repeated her message, "SEAN—In store. Take Belle — HIDE!"

This time, Micah understood her intent and, ducking his head furtively, returned to the burro and quickly stashing the baskets in the weeds, he untied Belle and disappeared around the side of the building.

Jessie's legs were weak with relief for Micah and fear for herself. Then she realized that she had been repeating the Scripture, "What time I am afraid, I will trust in Thee.... What time I am afraid, I will trust in Thee...." over and over again.

Over her quoting, she now heard Sean's conversation with Otis.

"Yeah, I thought I would come up and spend a little time in your neck of the woods, so to speak." Sean's small laugh had that wicked lilt to it that had always thrown dread into Jessie's heart.

"Thought I might look up an uncle of mine that used to live somewhere near here," Sean continued.

"Yeah." Otis had a strange reserve in his tone. "Jest who maught thet be?"

"Man by the name of Charlie McAllister."

Jessie suddenly realized that she had been frozen into one position for several minutes now and not wanting to arouse suspicion of any sort, she turned to the side and began to methodically place articles into her basket, not even realizing just what she was adding to her previous selections.

There had been a long pause and then Sean cleared his throat again, "Now I haven't seen Uncle Charlie for years, but he used to live in these parts."

Still Otis did not answer.

"Like I said," began Sean again, "it's been a while since I've been here and I thought you might be willing to give me directions to his house. You know, things have changed a bit since I was here before and all," Sean finished lamely.

Jessie could just see Otis stroking his chin as he slowly made his response, "Weil, now, Charlie McAllister, did ye say?"

Jessie knew Sean well enough to know that Otis' slow response had to have been killing him. If Otis had been a smaller man, Sean might have chosen to grab him by the collar and hasten his response. As it was, however, Sean's tension was palpable.

"Seems t' me there's a feller named thet whut lived near here sum tim' ago," Otis had continued and Jessie imagined the appraising look that he must be giving Sean.

"Don't think nobidy's seen 'im fer a while, now's I recollect," Otis continued in his interminably slow way.

Jessie heard the stream of spit that hit Otis' spittoon and she could only imagine that Sean must be white-knuckled with rage by now.

"What do you mean, nobody's seen him…did he move away?" Sean pressed between clenched teeth.

"Folks don't rightly know. Maught hev moved. Maught not." Jessie could feel Sean's anger rising to the surface now.

"Well, old man, looks like I'll just have to go to his house and see…."

Otis interrupted, "Ya won't fin' no house, boy," emphasis on the boy.

"What do you mean?" Sean asked, obviously still clenching his teeth.

"I mean this Mister McAllister, yer Uncle, din't live in no house."

"What did he do? Live in a hole in the ground?" Sean asked sarcastically.

"Don't rightly know," Otis delivered quietly. "He'as a loner… lived up with' th' bears an' bobcats and painters…some say they jest spirited him away…."

"That's nonsense!" Sean ejaculated with unrestrained annoyance now.

"'Peers t' me, ye'd do weil t' learn better minners, boy," Otis fairly spat out and then did spit a long stream into his spittoon, once again.

"Even iffen this Charlie McAllister is yer uncle, he jest maught taken a notion to shoot ya iffen ya go messin' around on his property. Folks 'round here don't take too kindly to trispassers. They's mor'n one shaller grave 'round here…."

Jessie could feel the cold, hard stare that her uncle gave to Otis.

But Jessie, also, knew that her uncle was really a coward at heart.

Otis had made his point.

The screen door suddenly slammed and Jessie jumped out of her skin as Sean apparently had left without saying another word. Moments later his old pickup roared to life and spun out of the gravel parking lot. Jessie wanted to run see which direction he had headed in but knew that would arouse too much attention.

Also, in the palpable silence that followed, Jessie realized that she had been shaking and that her knees felt like water, so the desire to see would have been just that—a desire with the inability to follow it up with action. The urge to sit was almost overpowering, but gradually Jessie found the strength to stand upright. She leaned against the post at the end of the aisle and took several deep breaths to calm her nerves.

"Ya need any he'p wid yer shoppin', Zeke," and Jessie suddenly realized that Otis was addressing her.

She peered around the end of the aisle only to hear herself say in a squeaky voice, "Oh, I'm doing all right with it. Just making sure I've got everything."

"Yer'es white as a sheet, boy!" Otis exclaimed. "Thet li'l alticashun upset ya, did it? Weil, ya gotta toughen up, son, iffen yer gonna live 'round here. Them types come 'round ever now an' then in life. Ya' gotta learn ta' take th' bad wid' th' good, but iffen he's ole Charlie's nep'hew, I'm a monkey's uncle!" Jessie felt that her gulp was surely audible.

"Say, whur's thet brother of yor'n?" Otis suddenly queried.

"Ah...he should be along any minute...." Jessie replied lamely. "He's just tending to Belle."

"She givin' 'im problems?" Otis continued.

"Uh...no...uh...we brought some baskets for you to look at, too, and maybe the ropes are giving him trouble," Jessie, thinking quickly and not wanting to lie, had replied.

Moments later, Micah entered the store laden with the baskets.

He, too, looked a little pale and this was not lost on Otis. "Morning, son. Them ropes giving you fits?" Otis quizzed as he narrowed his eyes and took in the significant glances exchanged between the two teenagers.

"Ropes...." Micah began.

Jessie shot him a pleading look and Micah continued. "Yeah, that's what I get for letting my brother tie them on." And Micah shook his head and rolled his eyes for effect.

"Weil, let's see whut ya got!" Otis exclaimed.

Micah laid the baskets on the counter and withdrew the carvings.

"Weil, now, this ain't bad work. Maught be able to do sumpin' wid these at thet."

Dickering ensued and soon Otis was placing the baskets and carvings around his store, and Jessie and Micah were breathing a huge sigh of relief. Their joy, however, in finding a point of revenue was overshadowed by the presence of Sean in Macon County. They would certainly have to be careful on their way back home.

Jessie quickly finished up their shopping, adding more purchases than they had planned, so that they would not have to return again anytime soon. Then she and Micah left the general store under Otis Sneed's still inquisitive stare. Jessie signed furtively to Micah on their departure asking if Micah had noticed which way Sean had gone. Micah signed that Sean had gone in the opposite direction from the cabin. Relieved for the moment, Jessie knew that none-the-less, they would have to be a lot more careful in the future.

As the two disappeared around the corner of the building, taking care to stay just off the road and out of sight of any vehicles, Pop Caruthers entered the store.

"Say, Otis, who wuz thet who peeled out in sech a hurry a whaile back?"

"Oh, jest some jerk, who'as lookin' fer Charlie McAllister?"

"Ya' tell 'im inythin'?"

"Whut ya' take me fer, Pop? Sum dang fool?" Otis asked irritably.

"Weil, who wuz it then?" Pop continued.

"Sumbidy claimin' to be a neffew of Charlie's, but thet boy wern't no relation of Charlie's, I kin tell ya' thet."

"Who d'ya' think it wuz, then?" Pop pressed.

"Don't rightly know, but his presence here seemed a maught diskinsertin' to them two young boys...." Otis said, stroking his chin and musing as he spoke. "Now, thet kinnecshun, I'd like ta know sumthin' about!"

Chapter Twenty

The trip back to the cabin was different from any other trip that had been made yet. The siblings found themselves constantly looking over their shoulders and talking in whispers. The beauty of the trail, with the wild flowers blooming in profusion, was scarcely noticed as both of the youngsters mused over the events of the morning.

Both Jessie and Micah were relieved to know that Sean had survived the blow to his head without any obvious physical repercussions. At least they knew now, and could put their minds to rest over that concern. The fact that he had come looking for Uncle Charlie could only mean one thing, however. He was trying to locate them and that had raised fear in both hearts. They tried, all the way up the mountain, to put their fears at rest by trusting in the Lord. It was, indeed, a true struggle to walk by faith in this matter they found.

When they finally reached the pasture and tied Belle loosely to their staking tree, both teenagers looked at each other as a new realization hit them. Sean could have easily discovered them as they picnicked carelessly in this field only a short time ago. Jessie determined right then that they would have to be far more careful in the future.

It was agreed that Micah would stay behind and watch over Belle until Wolf came to get her, just in case Sean should find his way to Uncle Charlie's property. It was with some trepidation that Jessie left Micah and continued on through the tunnel.

What if Sean should discover Micah and Belle before they could be safely hidden on the back side of the mountain?

As Jessie made her way through the tunnel, she suddenly remembered Sarah's dream about the rattler turning into Uncle Sean. Could that have been some kind of a warning that had been given to them? She would pay more heed to those kinds of things in the future. She did believe that God still gave His people symbolic dreams and she would just have to be more attentive to His leading on a daily basis now. They could so easily have been caught in the store earlier. It made Jessie's skin crawl to think just how close a call that had been.

Upon attaining the cabin, Jessie struggled to assume a normal expression of joy to be returning to her family once more. She hurriedly provided the information that Micah was simply staying behind with Belle for a little while. Then she dropped her pack and her eyes so that Sarah would not see anything there. She rummaged around until she found the small bag of candy for the kids and while they were thus occupied and Sarah unpacked the knapsack, she motioned with her head for Grandpa to join her outside.

"I will let Wolf out and make sure he goes to get Belle, then I will be right back," she announced to the noisy scene before her. Grandpa followed her out the door and watched as she commanded Wolf to go fetch Belle. The dog looked at her for one brief moment, then left to do her bidding.

"What has happened, Jessie?" Grandpa asked quietly, concern written on his wrinkled brow.

"Sean...." Jessie began. "Sean came into the general store while I was shopping."

Grandpa's eyes widened as he asked in a hushed voice, laced with concern, "Did he see you?"

"No, and I was able to gain Micah's attention so that he didn't see him either, but he was asking about Uncle Charlie," Jessie looked soberly into her grandpa's eyes to read any fear that might be registered there.

After relaying the whole of the incident to her grandpa, Jessie looked to him for wisdom on the matter. Grandpa just stood there thoughtfully as he watched Wolf gain the ridge of the mountain, then disappear out of sight. Still he said nothing.

Jessie was beginning to wonder if he would respond at all, when he took a deep breath and uttered, "Jessie we need to keep everyone on this side of the mountain until we believe that the danger has truly passed. If Sean went in the direction of town, as you say he did, then he may go to the courthouse and check out the location of Charlie's property. He may well hike up here and look around. The odds of his finding Charlie's cabin are almost nil, but we need to do what we can to ensure that he never finds this place. We will light the fire only late at night and do our cooking and water heating then. We'll have to tell everyone to keep quiet for the time being and, while I understand your reluctance to tell Sarah and the children, I see no way around telling them. We will just pray that Sarah will handle it well."

"If that is what you think, Grandpa, then we will just have to do the best that we can and leave the rest in God's hands," Jessie replied, as she tried hard to cover her uneasiness that Sean might, indeed, discover the location of Charlie's property.

The two reentered the cabin to tell the noisy crew that for the next week or so they would be playing a game to discover just how quiet everyone could be. Sarah looked at them jauntily as if to say, "I know who the winner of this game will be!" but sobered when she saw Jessie signing to her and Josh to follow her into their bedroom.

Sarah's face turned pale at mention of Sean, but she then made a great effort to pull from down deep and face this new challenge with faith in God to protect them all. "Had He not been doing this all along, anyway?" she asked herself.

Josh simply received the news in his matter-of-fact Josh way. He promised to be the "King of Quiet" and Jessie believed that he would be just that.

Blessedly, Sarah already had their supper ready, so she was not too chagrined when the fire was allowed to go out. She just fell to planning their meals using the allotted time of cooking, from midnight to 3 a.m. Also, Grandpa did not think that Jessie and Micah should make another trip off of the mountain for a couple of weeks, so the groceries would have to be stretched farther. The kudzu was coming up in profusion now so they would try cooking with this plant. With the way it grew here, they certainly should not starve if they could stomach eating it!

Soon, Belle could be seen being led down the steep rocky face of the mountain and a short while later, Micah appeared. He had double-checked the area for both his and Jessie's footprints and had lightly brushed the dust of the cave to hide any evidence that they had ever been there. He was told that his hunting and fishing would be put on hold for a couple of weeks and everyone was to remain in the perimeter of the cabin. So, once again, Sean was posing a threat to this happy family, but they simply would have to make it through this, too, and Micah, as he assumed a masculine stance, was determined that they would.

Two days later, as the children played quietly, Jessie went to the back door to throw the dishwater out on Sarah's flower garden. She noticed that Wolf kept looking to the top of the mountain and an unease came over her. Micah had noticed Wolf's behavior, too, and upon approaching the dog knelt beside him, caressing his soft fur and asking him softly what was wrong.

Jessie joined the two and Micah told her he thought he should check it out. She agreed but thought they should consult Grandpa first. Grandpa, too, thought that Micah should make a trip through the tunnel and listen carefully. Upon hearing nothing, he was to venture out slowly and see what he could see.

The plan laid, Micah began the venture with a now obviously worried Wolf being made to stay behind. Jessie remained at the door to the tunnel to listen out for any signs of trouble and Micah cautiously and quietly crept down the tunnel. Hearing nothing at the other end, Micah gently pushed the small boulder a fraction of an inch and listened again. Still hearing nothing, he continued pushing the boulder one fraction of an inch at a time until he could finally push his shoulders through the opening.

Cautiously making his way around the perimeter of the cave, in order to leave no footprints, he finally gained the entrance. By now, the spring growth had covered the entrance even better than before, making it very difficult to see unless one just stumbled upon it. Micah peered out cautiously through this growth and almost fell backwards in surprise.

There below him, at their picnic rock, was his uncle Sean, attempting to raise a tent! His heart beating in his throat, Micah cautiously approached the growth to gaze once more upon the scene. Sean appeared to be in a nasty mood and was obviously having difficulty with the erecting of his tent. As Micah continued to watch, Sean gave up momentarily on the tent and withdrew a roll of paper from the saddle of his horse. The animal shied away from Sean's touch and he swore at the creature. It whinnied pitifully and Micah felt remorse that it had fallen into Sean's hands.

Sean unrolled the paper and began perusing it intently. He looked up occasionally and, all in all, seemed to Micah to be getting his bearings. Soon, Sean went back to the erection of his tent and Micah slipped back to the entrance to the tunnel. He carefully replaced the small boulder and then began his trek back to the cabin, dreading all the while what he would be forced to reveal to his family.

Grandpa was deeply chagrined to learn that Sean was so close and to learn, too, that Micah had, also, noted a rifle strapped to the horse. All windows to the cabin were immediately closed and draped with blankets to cover any sounds that the baby might make. The little ones were told that they could no longer leave the cabin until further notice and Wolf was brought in to keep him from going to the staking tree, and bringing back Sean's horse!

Belle was relegated to being a barn burro and any and all activities which might produce excess noise were postponed indefinitely. Sarah was the surprise in all of this as she was exhibiting a great degree of calm. She fell to her tasks with greater vigor and assured all that God would, indeed, protect them. Jessie marveled at the transformation and thanked God for it as well.

Jessie firmly believed that they were well hidden and that it would take a miracle for Sean to find them, nevertheless, she well knew that God's ways are not our ways, and that if God allowed them to be discovered that He had a plan in it all.

Until their position had been threatened, however, she really had not realized just how happy they had all become here and that to give it up now would be a heartbreak to them for sure.

Nevertheless, Jessie wanted God's will done in their lives.

Chapter Twenty-One

The next morning found Micah quietly and cautiously making his way back to the mouth of the cave. He watched for thirty minutes before he finally saw Sean emerge from his tent. The man looked as if he had not slept well and his efforts at preparing his own breakfast did not appear to be going all that well. Poor Micah! He would love to go on down to the camp and help his uncle out, but he certainly knew better than to trust him—and after all, his own mother had said that Sean was not to know the object of their flight. He was bound, but in his heart he longed to help his uncle and for things to be right between them.

Sean soon proved to be in his usual foul temper and Micah felt for the poor horse. The mare could reach the little stream and had picked all the grass in the limited range of her lead, but Micah was sure she must be hungry. Sean soon finished his breakfast, having burned his hand in the process. He had wrapped it in his handkerchief as he issued fort a string of obscenities. His coffee burner lay where he had slung it in the grass after he had burned his hand on it.

Walking toward the edge of the mountain, Sean began calling Uncle Charlie. He kept his roll of paper in his good hand and surveyed it periodically as he called repeatedly for Charlie McAllister. Micah stuck to his outpost until Sean ventured too close for comfort, then he reentered the tunnel pulling the small boulder behind him.

Later in the afternoon, Micah resumed his post only to find Sean taking an afternoon nap with the horse still tied in the same position. He was surveying the scene when, to his dismay, he suddenly spied Wolf headed stealthily towards the horse. Micah rose to his haunches as if he could do something, then sank back down and realized that Wolf was on his own. Unbelievably, the horse stood docilely as Wolf worked to untie the lead. The horse followed Wolf obediently until Wolf started the ascent up the mountain, then she began her resistance. Wolf was no match for the strength of the mare when she decided that she would not climb the boulder strewn mountain. Soon, she broke free, and running with all her might, hit the trail for home.

The pounding of the horse's hooves on the rocks served to awaken Sean, who in a sleep-filled stupor climbed to his feet and began a jagged pursuit of the horse. Wolf hid behind a boulder, until Sean was out of sight, and then made for home following the path that only he knew.

Micah breathed a huge sigh of relief. Wolf had gone undetected and now the horse at least could find food. He hoped that Sean would not be able to catch it, but he felt pretty confident that the horse would not let Sean near him now that she was free.

After about thirty minutes, Sean returned to his camp in a murderous mood. He kicked out at everything in sight and was red in the face from his exertion. Then he started screaming for Uncle Charlie. He screamed until he became even redder in the face but to no avail. He picked up large stones and small boulders in his rage and repeatedly hurled them to the ground. Then he calmed down some and tried a different approach. He started whistling for the horse. After a while of this, Wolf apparently returned and hid behind another boulder. He started a mournful howling that totally disconcerted Sean. Micah's uncle looked about furtively and fearfully, then reached toward where the horse had been standing in order to retrieve his gun. It was only then that he realized that the horse had left with his gun. Sean's fear was palpable.

He glanced around and around and then looking at the sun, it must have occurred to him that he was facing a night alone on the mountain with no horse for a speedy exit and no gun. He hurriedly began dismantling the tent and packing his belongings. He winced repeatedly and cursed often from the pain in his hand. Then the mournful howling began again and Sean dropped things right and left as he strapped his pack to his back and hurried down the trail towards civilization.

Micah could have jumped for joy. Wait until he told everyone! Wolf had saved the day! Micah, was still careful not to leave any tracks and was careful to completely seal the tunnel entrance again, but he ran the length of the tunnel and broke in upon the group in the little cabin with the good news. The family had been worried when one of the kids had accidentally let Wolf out and he had taken off up the mountain. Now they could rejoice in his getaway. Wolf just could not break from his training of going and fetching a pack animal. How blessed they were, however, that this horse had not been willing to follow Wolf's leading. That could have spelled disaster!

As it was, however, the horse had pulled free from Wolf's grasp and had headed back to more civilized treatment. For this the family was eternally grateful and felt that the evening should be spent in celebration. They romped and played in the house and after a time, the blankets were taken from the windows and the fresh air was let in once more. A special supper was fixed and Wolf was, once again, given a hero's meal.

Micah kept watch for the next two weeks, but no trace of Sean was seen, so life returned to normal on the mountain. The garden had started coming in earnestly by now and the family feasted on the fresh vegetables. They had discovered they liked the taste of the kudzu and it was continually in ample supply.

As they started running low on staples, however, Micah and Jessie planned another trip down the mountain. They were anxious to stretch their legs again, so both looked forward to the trip with high spirits, though with some trepidation. Grandpa thought that Sean was surely long gone by now, but he still advised caution.

The evening before the trip found Sarah finishing up several more baskets and Grandpa working on smoothing a couple more carvings. Jessie and Micah went over their list again for the third time, while the younger ones scampered around their feet. Jessie suddenly realized that Sean's appearance on the mountain and his equally sudden departure had seemed to release a pressure valve, and the family felt safer than they had felt since before their mother's death.

The trip down the mountain the next day was simply marked by discovering more varieties of flowers in bloom and finding that the yellow Lady's Slippers were spent. Oh well, Jessie would just mark in her mind where they were located and bring Sarah to see them next year.

Otis seemed genuinely pleased to see the siblings again and was full of local gossip. After Micah and Jessie had shown him the new baskets and carvings, the proud store owner admitted that their items had shown appeal to the tourists who passed through and he was glad to get more of their work. Jessie breathed a huge sigh of relief at this news.

The next news, however, stopped her in her tracks. She suddenly realized that Otis was asking her if she remembered that jerk that had been in the store a couple of weeks ago. She slowly nodded her head in affirmation.

"Weil," Otis began slowly as he turned one of the carvings over in his hand examining it further, then looked at the teenagers with narrowed eyes, "that rascal cum back in a coupl'a days later. He 'ad rented a horse frum one o' th' local stables an he 'as headin' up ta Charlie McAllister's place. I warned 'im it 'as rough goin' but he weren't listening. I said 'as he orter watch 'isself er he'd git eat up by a snake er a painter er a coyot'. He 'lowed as he weren't 'fraid o' none o' those things an' he patted 'is rifle right smug-like."

Otis spat disgustedly, "City slickers, thets whut I calls em! Think 'as how they know so much! Inyhow, 'is horse he 'ad rented, hit got th' last laugh on 'im."

Guffawing so hard he had to hold his belly, Otis finished his tale, "'At horse, hit got loose sumhow an' headed back to wher's folks 'as got better minners. Hit left this rascal high an' dry. Ended up back at th' stable car'in th' saddle an' this bloke's rifle. I bet he weren't none too brave 'ithout hit! I'd loved ta heve seen thet sitiation unfold, now, thet'd been a sight ta see!"

Otis guffawed again so hard that he had to wipe the tears from his eyes with his big, grubby paws. "Yeah, now, thet'd been a sight ta see! Inyhow, thet feller ended up back 'ere all scratched an' burned an' red in th' face. He 'as mad as fire! Said he orter sue th' stable fer rentin' 'im sech a horse! Ol' man Crane, th' stable owner, tol' 'im iffen he iver caught 'im in these parts agin he'd think sue! 'Is horse 'as already gittin' saddle sores an' he'd only had 'im overnight. He must 'av left th' saddle on thet pore horse all night long! Crane 'as hoppin' mad hisself an' I thought the'd cum ta blows, but this city feller 'as all blow. He 'as lily-livered under all them words!"

"Weil, Crane got ta threatenin' 'im hisself and tol' 'im 'is life wouldn't be worth a plug nickel iffen he ever saw 'im around 'ere agin. This feller turned a li'l pale an' he skedaddled. Don't think we'll 'av to worry 'bout seein' 'im agin. He couldn't git outta 'ere fast enough! Charlie's nephew, my eye!" Otis spat again for effect.

Jessie stood, wide-eyed, taking it all in. She had turned kind of pale at mention of Sean's name, but now she felt pure joy welling up in her and like a young kid, she suddenly wanted to whoop and holler. Sean would not be returning. She knew this in her heart and she was elated. God had worked it all out and all they had to do was trust Him. "Wasn't He incredible!" she thought.

She and Micah hurriedly made their purchases, left their wares and started back up the mountain. They felt frisky as lambs and went up the road punching one another and laughing with relief and glee. They were free from that threat! Their minds could hardly take it in. Just wait until they told the others! And, thus went the rest of the day—in pure praise and unrestrained joy. The God, on whom they relied, had kept them safe and they would rejoice in this for a long time to come.

Chapter Twenty-two

The rest of the summer saw the family working hard in their gardens and laying up a goodly supply of food for the winter months to come. Sarah continued to make baskets, experimenting all the while by adding found materials such as feathers that the other children brought her. That way they felt like they were all contributing to the meager income.

Grandpa continued his carvings and gradually added walking sticks and wooden bowls to his craft. He even teamed up with Sarah and added some small carved nuts and animals to her baskets. Meanwhile Micah had sold the snakeskin for a goodly sum.

He and Josh were responsible for gathering the kudzu vines and harvesting the leaves and roots in order to extend their fare. They, also, continued their fishing and gathering of firewood for the winter months.

All in all, life was flowing along and their needs were being met. Jessie looked around one day and noticing the rosy cheeks of her siblings, realized just how healthy they all were. Even Grandpa had regained some of his agility and strength, and seemed the picture of health. They had so much for which to be thankful.

Fall came and the children raked up leaves to jump into. They gathered the last of the pears and made jar after jar of pear preserves. They gathered the late apples and placed the best ones carefully in the root cellar after making many jars of apple butter and some apple sauce with the rest. The boys found hazelnut, chinquapin, and walnut trees in the woods and brought home tow sacks full of the mouthwatering nutmeats. The tender young greens were picked and soon there would be turnips to harvest.

Both the Irish potatoes and sweet potatoes had done well and Josh's idea of planting gourds had paid off. Jessie and Micah had taken a load down the mountain recently and Otis had bought every one.

They had at least a dozen large pumpkins and several smaller ones along with butternut and acorn squash. The boys and Grandpa had taken Uncle Charlie's sickle and cut the hay in the field, tying it up in neat bundles for the livestock for the winter.

The chicks that they had hatched out were just beginning to lay and Jessie would soon get her wish of a fried egg for breakfast. The goat's milk did not yield an overabundance of butter fat, but they did get enough butter for seasoning. Jessie still would not allow herself the money to spend for tea and that she did miss. Grandpa had fixed sassafras tea and it was good, but Jessie still dreamed of drinking good, old-fashioned iced tea again one day.

Still and all, that was her only want. All else had been met and amply so.

Jessie had spent the summer perusing the woods looking for the ginseng that she hoped would eventually keep them clothed. She had located a number of areas where the plant grew in profusion. Now it was time to harvest.

Grandpa hiked with her when the day for harvesting came. He carefully dug through the soil and located each root and then showed Jessie the ones to harvest and the ones that still had more seasons to go. The two worked hard that day and only had a few roots to show for their labors. Jessie would go out on the morrow alone and hope for better results. Grandpa said that the roots would dry and thus weigh a lot less, but they would still bring a goodly sum and thus he and Jessie planned to keep a special watch on these plantings throughout the years, and make sure that the seeds were placed carefully in the ground. Both knew that someday this would be their main source of income if they were careful with their harvesting and planting.

Jessie returned after the second day with a little larger haul and Grandpa seemed particularly pleased. He threw his arm around Jessie, proclaiming that they were in the "sang" business now for sure. She smiled up at him and he offered to clean the roots while she got washed up.

Sarah had an excited look on her face and she motioned to Jessie to join her in the pantry after Jessie was through washing up. It did not take long for the older sister to understand why her sibling had asked that she join her. Sarah was proudly surveying the fruits of their labors.

There was row upon row and jar upon jar of fruits and vegetables. Colorful jars of canned tomatoes, pickles, okra, soup mixture, beans, asparagus, greens, cherries, peaches, pears, rhubarb, apples, grape juice, blackberry jelly, strawberry preserves, blueberry jam, tomato ketchup, applesauce, pear preserves, sauerkraut, cream-style corn, beets, carrots, Crowder peas, and pepper relish.

Then there were the jars of honey, the baskets of nuts, and the bins of their own ground cornmeal. The ceilings were hung with ropes of garlic and onions and a myriad of herbs which Grandpa had harvested from the woods. There were also some hot peppers which had come up volunteer and which they used for seasoning.

In the root cellar to which Sarah led her next were the potatoes, pumpkins, winter squash, some late tomatoes, apples, pears, carrots, and more onions. Grandpa may not be a craftsman of the same quality as his brother Charlie—however, he had proven that he had quite a green thumb. He had trained his grandchildren well in the art of gardening and now the girls were surveying the fruits of all of the family's hard work.

Sarah stood back with such a look of accomplishment and pride on her face that Jessie grabbed her and they swung around the yard in a crazy dance. This attracted the attention of the younger children and soon the yard was full of the whooping and hollering and wild cavorting of the children. They swung around and around and eventually fell in a wild heap in the pile of leaves.

Grandpa came to check out the commotion and laughed out loud at the sight. Wolf, of course, had to get in on the action and he barked and yipped like a young pup.

Eventually, the older girls were able to disentangle themselves from the leaves and the kids, and stood to pick the debris off of all of them. Jessie, still laughing, pulled leaves from her sibling's hair and swung the little ones once more into the air.

Finally, the wild frolic was over and the girls fell to the task of getting everyone fed. The blessing that night was rendered by Grandpa who was full of thanks for all that his Lord had provided, including the laughter and fun.

Thanksgiving Week found Grandpa and Micah winding their way through the woods looking for signs of turkey. There was such a stillness in the air, and the woods had taken on the gray hue of late autumn as the trunks and branches of the trees were exposed for all to see. Grandpa, especially, seemed to delight in the subtle shadings of gray of the different tree types. He took special effort to teach Micah how to tell one type of tree from the next just by observing their bark. Micah had quickly learned the hickory, oak, and maple. The young locust and sassafras saplings were also easy to identify, but some of the less common trees he was still learning and Grandpa proved to be a patient teacher.

Meanwhile, the girls were preparing to cook a feast. They were laying out their plans and getting all in readiness. Sarah's cheeks stayed a rosy hue in her excitement. She bustled around the tiny kitchen and dining area, periodically issuing requests to Josh to fetch various supplies from the pantry or root cellar, and keeping a close eye on the little ones, all at the same time.

Jessie eyed her younger sister with admiration. She was well suited to domesticity. On the other hand, Jessie longed to be out of doors traipsing through the woods with the men folk. How she loved the smell of the woods, the feel of her legs pumping to take her up the mountainside, the occasional sight of wildlife, identifying plants and trees, and digging in the soft earth for sang. She was well suited for her role and had handled with grace the responsibilities God had given her. Actually, they had all stepped into their roles without complaint.

Thanksgiving Day arrived and the little one's eyes opened wide with delight at the plump turkey, all golden brown, gracing the middle of their trestle table (built by Grandpa some months back). There were bowls filled with mashed potatoes, green beans, cream style corn, and fluffy biscuits. Pans of squash casserole, apple dumplings, and pumpkin pies rested on Uncle Charlie's original kitchen table, along with old fashioned butterscotch pies made with walnuts, Jessie's favorite. The only store-bought food item was a can of cranberry sauce, which Jessie had splurged and bought. Her mother had always said that Thanksgiving was not Thanksgiving without cranberry sauce and Jessie meant to carry on the tradition.

The family gathered around the table and sat down in their respective places, all but Sarah, who still stood, her big blue eyes shining. She clapped her hands for attention and then turned to their cupboard with her back to her family. When she turned back around to face everyone again, she was carrying, as if it were some great treasure—a tall glass of iced tea which she proudly placed before her sister, Jessie.

Jessie's eyes were brimming with tears as she saw the gift and looked into her sister's radiant face. Then Sarah deferred to Micah, who explained that he had found a large patch of Galax and had, at Grandpa's suggestion, picked some of the deep green leaves. On a supposed hunting trip, he had taken them to a local florist, who had bought the entire bunch and wanted more. So they now had another small source of income.

Grandpa, Sarah, and Micah had agreed that the money from the sale of this first bunch, however, would be used to buy something special for Jessie, in appreciation of all she had done for their family. She was now the proud owner of a small box of tea bags, which she could fix and enjoy whenever she chose.

The ice had been donated by Josh. He had climbed back under an overhang earlier this morning and discovered what he had been seeking—the first newly formed icicles from the past few cold days. Thus, Jessie could now enjoy a tall glass of real iced tea.

Jessie was truly overwhelmed by the gesture and as she looked around at each dear face, and saw the joy of giving shining out of their eyes. She wondered how she could have chosen to do otherwise than to care for them.

Noticing Jessie gulping hard and unable to respond, Grandpa cleared his throat and pointed out that today they would feast, indeed, but first they would give thanks. As they held hands around the table and Grandpa's voice was raised with special gratitude, Jessie lifted her eyes, looked Heavenward and in an instant seemed to see back through time. She caught her breath as she saw again her mother's radiant look on the day of her death. She had counted on God to see them through and He had. He had been with them every step of the way and as they continued their journey into the future, they could still count on Him for He was already there, in their future, providing for their every need. And, wherever her dad and her Uncle Charlie were, He was caring for them, too. As Grandpa continued his blessing of gratitude, Jessie prayed fervently for the safety of these two men, her dad and her great uncle, and that the mystery of their whereabouts would be resolved one day soon. She thanked her God, once again, for the fact that he had healed her grandfather's mind and that Grandpa had shared so freely all of his years of wisdom with his grandchildren. What a help and source of comfort he had been!

Jessie could barely contain the thankfulness that welled up in her heart and as the family breathed a collective, "Amen." Jessie clasped firmly the hands of the siblings on each side of her before letting go.

In her spirit, however, she clasped even more firmly the hand of God, from which she knew she would never let go, as she marched by His side into the unknown years ahead on Castleknob.

www.ingramcontent.com/pod-product-compliance
Lightning Source LLC
Chambersburg PA
CBHW031300090426
42742CB00007B/531